PENGUIN BO

# Everlasting Syllabub and the Art of Carving

HANNAH GLASSE (1708–1780) is the author of *The Art of Cookery Made Plain and Easy*, first published in 1747. A bestselling cookbook for over a hundred years, it gave plain and easy instructions for low-cost fine dining and revolutionized the meals of the middle classes. She is considered the 'mother of the dinner party' by Clarissa Dickson-Wright; her trademark dishes include curry and roast hare.

# Everlasting Syllabub and the Art of Carving

HANNAH GLASSE

PENGUIN BOOKS

PENGUIN BOOKS

Published by the Penguin Group

Penguin Group (USA) Inc., 375 Hudson Street, New York, New York 10014, USA
Penguin Group (Canada), 90 Eglinton Avenue East, Suite 700, Toronto, Ontario,
Canada M4P 2Y3 (a division of Pearson Penguin Canada Inc.)
Penguin Books Ltd, 80 Strand, London WC2R 0RL, England
Penguin Ireland, 25 St. Stephen's Green, Dublin 2, Ireland
(a division of Penguin Books Ltd)
Penguin Books Australia Ltd, 250 Camberwell Road, Camberwell, Victoria 3124,
Australia (a division of Pearson Australia Group Pty Ltd)
Penguin Books India Pvt Ltd, 11 Community Centre, Panchsheel Park,
New Delhi – 110 017, India
Penguin Group (NZ), 67 Apollo Drive, Rosedale, Auckland 0632, New Zealand
(a division of Pearson New Zealand Ltd)
Penguin Books (South Africa) (Pty) Ltd, 24 Sturdee Avenue, Rosebank,
Johannesburg 2196, South Africa

Penguin Books Ltd, Registered Offices: 80 Strand, London WC2R 0RL, England

*The Art of Cookery Made Plain and Easy* first published 1747
This extract first published in Great Britain in Penguin Books 2011
First published in the USA by Viking Studio, a member of
Penguin Group (USA) Inc. 2011
1 3 5 7 9 10 8 6 4 2

Cover design based on a pattern from a plate by the Bow Porcelain Factory,
1770. Porcelain painted with enamels, moulded and gilded. (Photograph copyright
© Victoria & Albert Museum.) Picture research by Samantha Johnson.
Lettering by Stephen Raw.

ISBN: 978–0–241–95789–9

www.penguin.com

Penguin Books is committed to a sustainable
future for our business, our readers and our
planet. This book is made from paper certified
by the Forest Stewardship Council.

# Contents

# To the Reader

I believe I have attempted a branch of Cookery, which nobody has yet thought worth their while to write upon: but as I have both seen, and found by experience, that the generality of servants are greatly wanting in that point, therefore I have taken upon me to instruct them in the best manner I am capable; and, I dare say, that every servant who can but read, will be capable of making a tolerable good cook, and those who have the least notion of Cookery cannot miss of being very good ones.

If I have not wrote in the high polite style, I hope I shall be forgiven; for my intention is to instruct the lower sort, and therefore must treat them in their own way. For example, when I bid them lard a fowl, if I should bid them lard with large lardoons, they would not know what I meant; but when I say they must lard with little pieces of bacon, they know what I mean. So in many other things in Cookery, the great cooks have such a high way of expressing themselves, that the poor girls are at a loss to know what they mean: and in all *Receipt Books* yet printed, there are such an odd jumble of things as would quite spoil a *good dish*; and indeed some things so extravagant, that it would be almost a shame to make use of them, when a *dish* can be made full as good, or better, without them. For example: when you entertain ten or twelve people, you shall use for a cullis, a leg of veal and a ham; which, with the other ingredients, makes it very expensive, and all this only to mix with other sauce. And again, the essence of ham for sauce to *one dish*; when I will prove it, for about three shillings I will make as rich and high a sauce as all that will be, when done. For example:

Take a large deep stew-pan, half a pound of ham, fat and lean together, cut the fat and lay it over the bottom of the pan; then take a pound of veal, cut it into thin slices, beat it well with the back of a knife, lay it all over the ham; then have six pennyworth of the coarse lean part of the beef cut thin, and well beat, lay a layer of it all over, with some carrot, then the lean of the ham cut thin and laid over that; then cut two onions and strew over, a bundle of sweet herbs, four or five blades of mace, six or seven cloves, a spoonful of all-spice or Jamaica pepper, half a nutmeg beat, a pigeon beat all to pieces, lay that all over, half an ounce of truffles and morels, then the rest of your beef, a good crust of bread toasted very brown and dry on both sides: you may add an old cock beat to pieces; cover it close, and let it stand over a slow fire two or three minutes, then pour on boiling water enough to fill the pan, cover it close, and let it stew till it is as rich as you would have it, and then strain off all that sauce. Put all your ingredients together again, fill the pan with boiling water, put in a fresh onion, a blade of mace, and a piece of carrot; cover it close, and let it stew till it is as strong as you want it. This will be full as good as the essence of ham for all sorts of fowls, or indeed most made dishes, mixed with a glass of wine, and two or three spoonfuls of catchup. When your first gravy is cool, skim off all the fat, and keep it for use.

This falls far short of the expence of a leg of veal and ham, and answers every purpose you want.

If you go to market, the ingredients will not come to above half a crown; or for about eighteen-pence you may make as much good gravy as will serve twenty people.

Take twelve-penny-worth of coarse lean beef, which will be six or seven pounds, cut it all to pieces, flour it well; take a quarter of a pound of good butter, put it into a little pot or large deep stew-pan, and put in your beef: keep stirring it, and when it begins to look a little brown, pour in a pint of boiling water; stir it all together, put in a large onion, a bundle of sweet herbs, two or three blades of mace, five or six cloves, a spoonful of all-spice, a crust of bread toasted, and a piece of carrot; then pour in four or five quarts of water, stir all together, cover close, and let it stew till it is as rich as you would have it; when enough, strain it off, mix it with two or three spoonfuls of catchup, and half a pint of white wine; then put all the ingredients together again, and put in two quarts of boiling water, cover it close, and let it boil till there is about a pint; strain it off well, add it to the first, and give it a boil together. This will make a great deal of good rich gravy.

You may leave out the wine, according to what use you want it for; so that really one might have a genteel entertainment for the price the sauce of one dish comes to; but if gentlemen will have *French* cooks, they must pay for *French* tricks.

A *Frenchman* in his own country will dress a fine dinner of twenty dishes, and all genteel and pretty, for the expence he will put an *English* lord to for dressing one dish. But then there is the little petty profit. I have heard of a cook that used six pounds of butter to fry twelve eggs; when every body knows (that understands cooking) that half a pound is full enough, or more than need be used: but then it

3

would not be *French*. So much is the blind folly of this age, that they would rather be imposed on by a *French* booby, than give encouragement to a good *English* cook!

I doubt I shall not gain the esteem of those gentlemen; however, let that be as it will, it little concerns me; but should I be so happy as to gain the good opinion of my own sex, I desire no more; that will be a full recompence for all my trouble: and I only beg the favour of every lady to read *my Book* throughout before they censure me, and then I flatter myself I shall have their approbation.

I shall not take upon me to meddle in the physical way farther than two receipts, which will be of use to the public in general, one is for the bite of a mad dog; and the other, if a man should be near where the plague is, be shall be in no danger; which, if made use of, will be found of very great service to those who go abroad.

Nor shall I take upon me to direct a lady in the œconomy of her family; for every mistress does, or at least ought to know, what is most proper to be done there; therefore I shall not fill *my Book* with a deal of nonsense of that kind, which I am very well assured none will have regard to.

I have indeed given some of my dishes *French* names to distinguish them, because they are known by those names: and where there is a great variety of dishes, and a large table to cover, so there must be a variety of names for them; and it matters not whether they be called by a *French*, *Dutch*, or *English* name, so they are good, and done with as little expence as the dish will allow of.

I shall say no more, only hope *my Book* will answer the ends I intend it for; which is to improve the servants, and save the ladies a great deal of trouble.

# I: Choosing Wisely

How to chuse all Kinds of Butcher's Meat, Poultry, Fish, Butter, Eggs, and Cheese.

### To choose Beef
If it be true ox-beef, it will have an open grain, and the fat, if young, of a crumbling, or oily smoothness, except it be the brisket and neck pieces, with such others as are very fibrous. The colour of the lean should be of a pleasant carnation red, the fat rather inclining to white than yellow, (which seldom proves good,) and the suet of a fine white.

Cow-beef is of a closer grain, the fat whiter, the bones less, and the lean of a paler colour. If it be young and tender, the dent you make with your finger by pressing it, will, in a little time, rise again.

Bull beef is of a more dusky red, a closer grain, and firmer than either of the former; harder to be indented with your finger, and rising again sooner. The fat is very gross and fibrous, and of a strong rank scent. If it be old it will be so very tough, that if you pinch it you will scarce make any impression in it. If it be fresh, it will be of a lively fresh colour; but if stale, of a dark dusky colour, and very clammy. If it be bruised, the part affected will look of a more dusky or blackish colour than the rest.

## Mutton and Lamb

Take some of the flesh between your fingers and pinch it; if it feels tender, and soon returns to its former place, it is young; but if it wrinkles, and remains so, it is old. The fat will also, easily separate from the lean, if it be young; but if old, it will adhere more firmly, and be very clammy and fibrous. If it be ram mutton, the fat will be spongy, the grain close, the lean rough, and of a deep red, and when dented by your finger will not rise again. If the sheep had the rot, the flesh will be palish, the fat a faint white, inclining to yellow; the meat will be loose at the bone, and, if you squeeze it hard, some drops of water, resembling a dew or sweat, will appear on the surface. [If it be a fore-quarter, observe the vein in the neck, for if it look ruddy, or of an azure colour, it is fresh; but if yellowish, it is near tainting, and if green, it is already so. As for the hind-quarter, smell under the kidney, and feel whether the knuckle be stiff or limber; for if you find a faint or ill scent in the former, or an unusual limberness in the latter, it is stale.] For choosing a lamb's head, mind the eyes; if they be sunk or wrinkled, it is stale; if plump and lively, it is new and sweet.

## Veal

Observe the vein in the shoulder; for if it be of a bright red, or looks blue, it is newly killed; but if greenish, yellowish, or blackish, or more clammy, soft, and limber than usual, it is stale. Also, if it has any green spots about it, it is either tainting, or already tainted. If it be wrapped in wet cloths, it is apt to be musty; therefore always observe to smell to it. The loin taints first under the kidney, and the flesh, when stale, will be soft and slimy. The neck and breast are first tainted at the upper end, and when so, will have a dusky, yellowish, or greenish appearance, and the sweetbread on the breast will be clammy. The leg, if newly killed, will be stiff in the joint; but if stale, limber, and the flesh clammy, intermixed with green or yellowish specks. The flesh of a bull-calf is firmer grained and redder than that of a cow-calf, and the fat more curdled. In choosing the head, observe the same directions as above given for that of the lamb.

## Pork

Pinch the lean between your fingers; if it breaks, and feels soft and oily, or if you can easily nip the skin with your nails, or if the fat be soft and oily, it is young; but if the lean be rough, the fat very spongy, and the skin stubborn, it is old. If it be a boar, or a hog gelded at full growth, the flesh will feel harder and rougher than usual, the skin thicker, the fat hard and fibrous, the lean of a dusky red, and of a rank scent. To know if it be fresh or stale, try the legs and hands at the bone, which comes out in the middle of the fleshy part, by putting in your finger; for as it first taints in those places, you may easily discover it by smelling to your finger; also the skin will be clammy and sweaty when stale, but smooth and cool when fresh.

## Brawn

The best method of knowing whether brawn be young or old, is by the extraordinary or moderate thickness of the rind, and the hardness or softness of it; for the thick and hard is old, but the moderate and soft is young. If the rind and fat be remarkably tender, it is not boar brawn, but barrow or sow.

## Dried Hams and Bacon

Take a sharp-pointed knife, run it into the middle of the ham, on the inside, under the bone, draw it out quickly and smell to it; if its flavour be fine and relishing, and the knife little daubed, the ham is sweet and good; but if, on the contrary, the knife be greatly daubed, has a rank smell, and a hogoo issues from the vent, it is tainted. Or you may cut off a piece at one end to look on the meat; if it appear white and be well scented, it is good; but if yellowish, or of a rusty colour, not well scented, it either is tainted or rusty, or at least will soon be so. A gammon of bacon may be tried in the same manner, and be sure to observe that the flesh sticks close to the bones, and the fat and lean to each other; for if it does not, the hog was not found. Take care also that the extreme part of the fat near the rind be white, for if that be of a dark-ish or dirty colour, and the lean pale and soft, with some streaks of yellow, it is rusty, or will soon be so.

## Venison

Try the haunches, shoulders, and fleshy parts of the sides with your knife, in the same manner as before directed for ham, and in proportion to the sweet or rank smell it is new or stale. With relation to the other parts, observe the colour of the meat; for if it be stale or tainted, it will be of a black colour, inter-mixed with yellowish or greenish specks. If it be old, the flesh will be tough and hard, the fat contracted, the hoofs large and broad, and the heel horny and much wore.


## OF POULTRY

### To know if a Capon be a true one or not,
### or whether it be young or old, new or stale

If a capon be young, his spurs will be short and blunt, and his legs smooth: if a true capon, it will have a fat vein on the side of the breast, a thick belly and rump, and its comb will be short and pale. If it be new, it will have a close hard vent; but if stale, an open loose vent.


### To choose a Cock or Hen Turkey,
### Turkey-Poults, &c

If the spurs of a turkey-cock are short, and his legs black and smooth, he is young; but if his spurs be long, and his legs pale and rough, he is old. If long killed, his eyes will be sunk into his head, and his feet feel very dry; but if fresh, his feet will be limber, and his eyes lively. For the hen, observe the same signs. If she be with egg, she will have an open vent; but if not, a close, hard vent. The same signs will serve to discover the newness or staleness of turkey-poults; and, with respect to their age, you cannot be deceived.


### A Cock, Hen, &c

If a cock be young, his spurs will be short and dubbed; (be sure to observe that they are not pared or scraped to deceive you;) but if sharp and standing out, he is old. If his vent be hard and close, it is a sign of his being newly killed; but if he be stale, his vent will be open. The same signs will discover whether a hen be new or stale; and if old, her legs and comb will be rough; but if young, smooth.

### To know if Chickens are new or stale
If they are pulled dry, they will be stiff when new; but when stale, they will be limber, and their vents green. If they are scalded, or pulled wet, rub the breast with your thumb or finger, and if they are rough and stiff, they are new; but if smooth and slippery, stale.

### To choose a Goose, Wild-Goose, and Bran-Goose
If the bill and foot be red, and the body full of hairs, she is old; but if the bill be yellowish, and the body has but few hairs, she is young. If new, her feet will be limber; but if stale, dry. Understand the same of a wild-goose, and bran-goose.

### Wild and tame Ducks
These fowls are hard and thick on the belly, when fat, but thin and lean, when poor; limber-footed when new; but dry-footed when stale. A wild duck may be distinguished from a same one, by its foot being smaller and reddish.

### Bustard
Observe the same rules in choosing this curious fowl, as those already given for the turkey.

### The Shuffler, Godwits, Marle, Knots, Gulls, Ruffs, Dotters, and Wheat-Ears

These birds, when new, are limber-footed; when stale, dry-footed: when fat, they have a fat rump; when lean, a close and hard one; when young, their legs are smooth; when old, rough.

### Pheasant Cock and Hen

The spurs of the pheasant cock, when young, are short and dubbed; but long and sharp when old; when new, he has a firm vent, when stale, an open and flabby one. The pheasant hen, when young, has smooth legs, and her flesh is of a fine and curious grain; but when old, her legs are rough, and her flesh hairy when pulled. If she be with egg, her vent will be open; if not, close. The same signs, as to newness or staleness, are to be observed as were before given for the cock.

### Heath and Pheasant Poults

The feet of these, when new, are limber, and their vents white and stiff; but when stale, are dry-sooted, their vents green, and if you touch it hard, will peel.

### Heath Cock and Hen

The newness or staleness of these are known by the same signs as the foregoing; but when young, their legs and bills are smooth; when old, both are rough.

### Woodcock and Snipe

These fowls are limber-footed when new; when stale, dry-footed: if fat, thick and hard; but if their noses are snotty, and their throats moorish and muddy, they are bad. A snipe, particularly, if fat, has a fat vein in the side under the wing, and in the vent feels thick.

## Partridge Cock or Hen
These fowls, when young, have black bills, and yellowish legs; when old, white bills and blueish legs; when new, a salt vent; when stale, a green and open one, which will peel with a touch; if they had fed lately on green wheat, and their crops be full, smell to their mouths, lest their crops be tainted.

## Doves or Pigeons, Plovers, &c
The turtle-dove is distinguished by a blueish ring round its neck, the other parts being almost white. The stock-dove exceeds both the wood-pigeon and ring-dove in bigness. The dove-house pigeons are red-legged when old: if new and fat, limber footed, and feel full in the vent; but when stale, their vents are green and slabby.

After the same manner you may choose the grey and green plover, fieldfare, thrush, mavis, lark, blackbird, &c.

## Teal and Widgeon
These, when new, are limber-footed; when stale, dry-footed; thick and hard on the belly, if fat; but thin and soft, if lean.

## Hare
If the claws of a hare are blunt and rugged, and the cleft in her lip spread much, she is old; but the opposite, if

young: if new and fresh killed, the flesh will be white and stiff; if stale, limber and blackish in many places. If the hare be young, the ears will tear like a sheet of brown paper; if old, they are dry and tough.

## Leveret

The newness or staleness may be known by the same signs as the hare; but in order to discover if it be a real leveret, feel near the foot on its fore leg; if you find there a knob or small bone, it is a true leveret; but if not, a hare.

## A Rabbit

If a rabbit be old, the claws will be very long and rough, and grey hairs intermixed with the wool; but if young, the claws and wool smooth; if stale, it will be limber, and the flesh will look blueish, having a kind of slime upon it; but if fresh, it will be stiff, and the flesh white and dry.

# OF FISH

## To choose Salmon, Trout, Carp, Tench, Pike, Graylings, Barbel, Chub, Whiting, Smelt, Ruff, Eel, Shad, &c

The newness or staleness of these fish is known by the colour of their gills, their being hard or easy to be opened, the standing out or sinking of their eyes, their fins being stiff or limber, and by smelling to their gills. Eels taken in running water are better than those taken in ponds; of these, the silver ones are most esteemed.

## Turbot

If this fish be plump and thick, and its belly of a cream colour, it is good; but if thin, and of a blueish white on the belly, not so.

## Soals

If these are thick and stiff, and of a cream colour on the belly, they will spend firm; but if thin, limber, and their bellies of a blueish white, they will eat very loose.

## Plaice and Flounders

When these fish are new, they are stiff, and the eyes look lively and stand out; but when stale, the contrary. The best plaice are blueish on the belly; but flounders of a cream colour.

## Cod and Codling

Choose those which are thick towards the head, and their flesh, when cut, very white.

## Fresh Herrings and Mackerel

If these are new, their gills will be of a lively shining redness, their eyes sharp and full, and the fish stiff; but if stale, their gills will look dusky and faded, their eyes dull and sunk down, and their tails limber.

## Pickled Salmon

The scales of this fish, when new and good, are stiff and shining, the flesh oily to the touch, and parts in flakes without crumbling; but the opposite, when bad.

## Pickled and Red Herrings

Take the former, and open the back to the bone; if it be white, or of a bright red, and the flesh white, oily, and fleaky, they are good. If the latter smell well, be of a good gloss, and part well from the bone, they are also good.

## Dried Ling

The best sort of dried ling is that which is thickest in the pole, and the flesh of the brightest yellow.

## Pickled Sturgeon

The veins and gristle of the fish, when good, are of a blue colour, the flesh white, the skin limber, the fat underneath of a pleasant scent, and you may cut it without its crumbling.

## Lobsters

If a lobster be new, it has a pleasant scent at that part of the tail which joins to the body, and the tail will, when opened, fall smart, like a spring; but when stale, it has a rank scent, and the tail limber and flagging. If it be spent, a white scurf will issue from the mouth and roots of the small legs. If it be full, the tail, about the middle, will be full of hard reddish skinned meat, which you may discover by thrusting a knife between the joints, on the bend of the tail. The heaviest are best, if there be no water in them. The cock is generally smaller than the hen, of a deeper red when boiled, has no spawn or seed under its tail, and the uppermost fins within its tail are stiff and hard.

### Crab fish, great and small

When they are stale, their shells will be of a dusky red colour, the joints of their claws limber; they are loose, and may be turned any way with the finger, and from under their throat will issue an ill smell; but if otherwise, they are good.

### Prawns and Shrimps

If they are hard and stiff, of a pleasant scent, and their tails turn strongly inward, they are new; but if they are limber, their colour faded, of a faint smell; and feel slimy, they are stale.

## OF BUTTER, EGGS, AND CHEESE

### To choose Butter and Eggs

When you buy butter, taste it yourself at a venture, and do not trust to the taste they give you, lest you be deceived by a well-tasted and scented piece artfully placed in the lump. Salt butter is better scented than tasted, by putting a knife into it, and putting it immediately to your nose; but, if it be a cask, it may be purposely packed, therefore trust not to the top alone, but unhoop it to the middle, thrusting your knife between the staves of the cask, and then you cannot be deceived.

When you buy eggs, put the great end to your tongue; if it feels warm, it is new; but if cold, it is stale; and according to the heat or coldness of it, the egg is newer or staler. Or take the egg, hold it up against the sun or a candle; if the white appears clear and fair, and the yolk round, it is good; but if muddy or cloudy, and the yolk broken, it is bad. Or take the egg, and put it into a pan of cold water; the fresher it is, the sooner it will sink to the bottom; but if it be rotten, or addled, it will swim on the surface of the water. The best way to keep them is in bran or meal; though some place their small ends downwards in fine wood-ashes. But for longer keeping, burying them in salt will preserve them almost in any climate.

## Cheese

Cheese is to be chosen by its moist and smooth coat; if old cheese be rough-coated, rugged or dry at top, beware of little worms or mites; if it be over-full of holes, moist or spungy, is subject to maggots. If any soft or perished place appear on the outside, try how deep it goes, for the greater part may be hid within.

# II: The Art of Carving

## To cut up a Turkey

Raise the leg, open the joint, but be sure not to take off the leg; lace down both sides of the breast, and open the pinion of the breast, but do not take it off; raise the merry-thought between the breast-bone and the top; raise the brawn, and turn it outward on both sides, but be careful not to cut it off, nor break it; divide the wing pinions from the joint next the body, and stick each pinion where the brawn was turned out; cut off the sharp end of the pinion, and the middle-piece will fit the place exactly. A bustard, capon, or pheasant, is cut up in the same manner.

## To rear a Goose

Cut off both legs in the manner of shoulders of lamb; take off the belly-piece close to the extremity of the breast; lace the goose down both sides of the breast, about half an inch from the sharp bone: divide the pinions and the flesh first laced with your knife, which must be raised from the bone, and taken off with the pinion from the body; then cut off the merry-thought, and cut another slice from the breast-bone, quite through; lastly turn up the carcase, cutting it asunder, the back above the loin-bones.

## To unbrace a Mullard or Duck

First, raise the pinions and legs, but cut them not off; then raise the merry-thought from the breast, and lace it down both sides with your knife.

## To unlace a Coney

The back must be turned downward, and the apron divided from the belly; this done, slip in your knife between the kidneys, loosening the flesh on each side; then turn the belly, cut the back cross-ways between the wings, draw your knife down both sides of the back-bone, dividing the sides and leg from the back. Observe not to pull the leg too violently from the bone when you open the side, but with great exactness lay open the sides from the scut to the shoulder; and then put the legs together.

## To wing a Partridge or Quail

After having raised the legs and wings, use salt and powdered ginger for sauce.

## To allay a Pheasant or Teal

This differs in nothing from the foregoing, but that you must use salt only for sauce.

## To dismember a Heron

Cut off the legs, lace the breast down each side, and open the breast-pinion, without cutting it off; raise the merry-thought between the breast-bone and the top of it; then raise the brawn, turning it outward on both sides; but break it not, nor cut it off; fever the wing-pinion from the joint nearest the body, sticking the pinions in the place where the brawn was; remember to cut off the sharp end of the pinion, and supply the place with the middle-piece.

In this manner some people cut up a capon or pheasant, and likewise a bittern, using no sauce but salt.

### To thigh a Woodcock
The legs and wings must be raised in the manner of a fowl, only open the head for the brains. And so you thigh curlews, plover, or snipe, using no sauce but salt.

### To display a Crane
After his legs are unfolded, cut off the wings; take them up, and sauce them with powdered ginger, vinegar, salt, and mustard.

### To lift a Swan
Slit it fairly down the middle of the breast, clean through the back, from the neck to the rump; divide it in two parts, neither breaking nor tearing the flesh; then lay the halves in a charger, the slit sides downwards; throw salt upon it, and set it again on the table. The sauce must be chaldron served up in saucers.

# III: Boiling and Dressing

That professed cooks will find fault with me for touching upon a branch of Cookery which they never thought worth their notice, is what I expect: however, this I know, it is the most necessary part of it; and few servants there are that know how to boil and dress to perfection.

## TO DRESS GREENS, ROOTS, &C

Always be very careful that your greens be nicely picked and washed. You should lay them in a clean pan, for fear of sand or dust which is apt to hang round wooden vessels. Boil all your greens in a copper or sauce-pan, by themselves, with a great quantity of water. Boil no meat with them, for that discolours them. Use no iron pans, &c. for they are not proper; but let them be copper, brass, or silver.

Most people spoil garden things by over-boiling them. All things that are green should have a little crispness, for if they are over-boiled, they neither have any sweetness or beauty.

### To dress Spinage

Pick it very clean, and wash it in five or six waters; put it in a sauce-pan that will just hold it, throw a little salt over it, and cover the pan close. Do not put any water in, but shake the pan often. You must put your sauce-pan on a clear quick fire. As soon as you find the greens are shrunk and fallen to the bottom, and that the liquor which comes out of them boils up, they are enough. Throw the spinage into a clean sieve to drain, and squeeze it well between two plates, and cut it in any form you like. Lay it in a plate, or small dish, and never put any butter on it, but put it in a cup or boat.

## To dress Cabbage, &c

Cabbage, and all sorts of young sprouts, must be boiled in a great deal of water. When the stalks are tender, or fall to the bottom, they are enough; then take them off, before they lose their colour. Always throw salt in your water before you put your greens in. Young sprouts you send to table just as they are, but cabbage is best chopped and put into a sauce-pan with a good piece of butter, stirring it for about five or six minutes, till the butter is all melted, and then send it to table.

## To dress Carrots

Let them be scraped very clean, and when they are enough, rub them in a clean cloth, then slice them into a plate, and pour some melted butter over them. If they are young spring carrots, half an hour will boil them; if large, an hour; but old Sandwich carrots will take two hours.

## To dress Turnips

They eat best boiled in the pot with the meat, and, when enough, which you will know by trying them with a fork, take them out and put them in a pan, and mash them with butter, a little cream, and a little salt, and send them to table. But you may do them thus: pare your turnips and cut them into dice, as big as the top of one's finger; put them into a clean sauce-pan, and just cover them with water. When enough, throw them into a sieve to drain, and put them into a sauce-pan with a good piece of butter and a little cream; stir them over the fire for five or six minutes, and send them to table.

### To dress Parsnips

They should be boiled in a great deal of water, and when you find they are soft, (which you will know by running a fork into them,) take them up, and carefully scrape all the dirt off them, and then with a knife scrape them all fine, throwing away all the sticky parts, and send them up plain in a dish with melted butter.

### To dress Broccoli

Strip all the little branches off till you come to the top one, then with a knife peel off all the hard outside skin, which is on the stalks and little branches, and throw them into water. Have a stew-pan of water with some salt in it; when it boils put in the broccoli, and when the stalks are tender it is enough, then send it to table with a piece of toasted bread soaked in the water the broccoli is boiled in under it, the same way as asparagus, with butter in a cup. The French eat oil and vinegar with it.

### To dress Potatoes

You must boil them in as little water as you can, without burning the sauce-pan. Cover the sauce-pan close, and when the skin begins to crack they are enough. Drain all the water out, and let them stand covered for a minute or two; then peel them, lay them in your plate, and pour some melted butter over them. The best way to do them is, when they are peeled to lay them on a gridiron till they are of a fine brown, and send them to table. Another way is to put them into a sauce-pan with some good beef dripping, cover them close, and shake the sauce-pan often for fear of burning to the bottom. When they are of a fine brown, and crisp, take them up in a plate, then put them into another for fear of the fat, and put butter in a cup.

## To dress Cauliflowers

Take your flowers, cut off all the green part, and then cut the flowers into four, and lay them into water for an hour; then have some milk and water boiling, put in the cauliflowers, and be sure to skim the sauce-pan well. When the stalks are tender, take them carefully up, and put them into a cullender to drain; then put a spoonful of water into a clean stew-pan with a little dust of flour, about a quarter of a pound of butter, and shake it round till it is all finely melted, with a little pepper and salt; then take half the cauliflower and cut it as you would for pickling, lay it into the stew-pan, turn it, and shake the pan round. Ten minutes will do it. Lay the stewed in the middle of your plate, and the boiled round it. Pour the butter you did it in over it, and send it to table.

## To boil them in the common Way

Cut the cauliflower stalks off, leave a little green on, and boil them in spring water and salt; about fifteen minutes will do them. Take them out and drain them; send them whole in a dish, with some melted butter in a cup.

## To dress French Beans
First string them, then cut them in two, and afterwards across; but if you would do them nice, cut the bean into four, and then across, which is eight pieces. Lay them into water and salt, and when your pan boils put in some salt and the beans; when they are tender they are enough; they will be soon done. Take care they do not lose their fine green. Lay them in a plate, and have butter in a cup.

## To dress Artichokes
Wring off the stalks, and put the artichokes into cold water, and wash them well, then put them in, when the water boils, with the tops downwards, that all the dust and sand may boil out. An hour and a half will do them.

## To dress Asparagus
Scrape all the stalks very carefully till they look white, then cut all the stalks even alike, throw them into water, and have ready a stew-pan boiling. Put in some salt, and tie the asparagus in little bundles. Let the water keep boiling, and when they are a little tender take them up. If you boil them too much you lose both colour and taste. Cut the round of a small loaf, about half an inch thick, toast it brown on both sides, dip it in the asparagus liquor, and lay it in your dish; pour a little butter over the toast, then lay your asparagus on the toast all round the dish, with the white tops outward. Do not pour butter over the asparagus, for that makes them

greasy to the fingers, but have your butter in a basin, and send it to table.

## To boil green Pease

Shell your pease just before you want them, put them into a very small quantity of boiling water, with a little salt and a lump of loaf sugar, when they begin to dent in the middle they are enough, strain them in a sieve, put a good lump of butter into a mug or small dish, give your pease a shake up with the butter, put them on a dish, and send them to table. Boil a sprig of mint in another water, chop it fine, and lay it in lumps round the edge of your dish.

## To dress Beans and Bacon

When you dress beans and bacon, boil the bacon by itself and the beans by themselves, for the bacon will spoil the colour of the beans. Always throw some salt into the water, and some parsley, nicely picked. When the beans are enough, (which you will know by their being tender,) throw them into a cullender to drain. Take up the bacon and skin it; throw some raspings of bread over the top, and if you have an iron, make it red hot and hold over it, to brown the top of the bacon; if you have not one, hold it to the fire to brown; put the bacon in the middle of the dish, and the beans all round, close up to the bacon, and send them to table, with parsley and butter in a basin.

# IV: The Hare and the Tortoise, Plus Other Mains

### Jugged Hare

Cut it into little pieces, lard them here and there with little slips of bacon, season them with Cayenne pepper and salt, put them into an earthen jug, with a blade or two of mace, an onion stuck with cloves, and a bundle of sweet herbs; cover the jug or jar you do it in so close that nothing can get in, then set it in a pot of boiling water, and three hours will do it; then turn it out into the dish, and take out the onion and sweet herbs, and send it to table hot. If you do not like it larded, leave it out.

### To jug a Hare, a second Way – An excellent Receipt

Cut a hare to pieces, but do not wash it; season it with an onion shred fine, rhyme, parsley, favoury, marjoram, lemon-peel, pepper, salt, and half a nutmeg; strew all these over your hare, slice some fat bacon thin, then put the hare into an earthen jug, without any water, and put a layer of hare and a layer of bacon; stop it close with a cloth tied on, and cover it with a tile, put it in a pot of cold water, and let it boil three hours. When you take it up, shake in some fresh butter till it is melted; garnish with lemon.

## TURTLE, MOCK-TURTLE, &C

### To dress a Turtle the West India Way

Take the turtle out of water the night before you dress it, and lay it on its back, in the morning cut its head off, and hang it up by its hind-fins for it to bleed till the blood is all out; then cut out the callapee (which is the belly) round, and raise it up; cut as much meat to it as you can; throw it into spring-water with a little salt, cut the fins off and scald them with the head; take off all the scales, cut all the white meat out and throw it into spring-water and salt; the guts and lungs must be cut out; wash the lungs very clean from the blood; then take the guts and maw and slit them open, wash them very clean, and put them on to boil in a large pot of water, and boil them till they are tender; then take off the inside skin, and cut them in pieces of two or three inches long. Have ready a good veal broth made as follows: take one large or two small knuckles of veal and put them on in three gallons of water; let it boil, skim it well, season with turnips, onions, carrots, and celery, and a good large bundle of sweet herbs; boil it till it is half wasted, then strain it off. Take the fins and put them in a stew-pan, cover them with veal broth, season with an onion chopped fine, all sorts of sweet herbs chopped very fine, half an ounce of cloves and mace, half a nutmeg beat very fine, stew it very gently till tender; then take the fins out, and put in a pint of Madeira wine, and stew it for fifteen minutes; beat up the whites of fix eggs, with the juice of two lemons; put the liquor in and boil it up, run it through a flannel bag, make it hot, wash the fins very clean and put them in. Take a piece of butter and put at the bottom of a stew-pan, put your white meat in, and sweat it gently till it is almost tender. Take the lungs and heart and cover them with veal broth, with an onion, herbs, and spice; as for the fins, stew them till tender; take out the lungs, strain the liquor off, thicken it, and put in a bottle of Madeira wine, season with Cayenne pepper and salt pretty high; put in the lungs and white meat, stew them up gently for fifteen minutes; have some force-meat balls made out of the white part instead of veal, as for Scotch collops: if the turtle has any eggs, scald them; if not, take twelve hard yolks of eggs, made into egg-balls; have your callapash, or deep shell, done round the edges with paste, season it in the inside with Cayenne pepper and salt, and a little Madeira wine, bake it half an hour, then put in the lungs and white meat, force-meat, and eggs over, and bake it half an hour; take the bones, and three quarts of veal broth, seasoned with an onion, a bundle of sweet herbs, two blades of mace, stew it an hour, strain it through a sieve, thicken it with flour and butter, put in half a pint of Madeira wine, stew it half an hour; season with Cayenne pepper and salt to your liking: this is the soup. Take the callapee, run your knife between the meat and shell, and fill it full of force-meat; season it all over with sweet herbs chopped fine, a shalot chopped, Cayenne pepper and salt, and a little Madeira wine; put a paste round the edge, and bake it an hour and a half; take the guts and maw, put them in a stew-pan, with a little broth, a bundle of sweet herbs, two blades of mace beat fine; thicken with a little butter rolled in flour; stew them gently for half an hour, season with Cayenne pepper and salt, beat up the yolks of two eggs in half a pint of cream, put it in, and keep stirring it one way till it boils up; then dish them up as follows:

Callapee.

Fricassee.    Soup.    Fins.

Callapash.

The fins eat fine when cold, put by in the liquor.

## To make a Curry the Indian Way

Take two small chickens, skin them and cut them as for a fricassee, wash them clean, and stew them in about a quart of water for about five minutes, then strain off the liquor and put the chickens in a clean dish; take three large onions, chop them small and fry them in about two ounces of butter, then put in the chickens and fry them together till they are brown; take a quarter of an ounce of turmeric, a large spoonful of ginger and beaten pepper together, and a little salt to your palate, strew all these ingredients over the chickens whilst frying, then pour in the liquor and let it stew about half an hour, then put in a quarter of a pint of cream and the juice of two lemons, and serve it up. The ginger, pepper, and turmeric must be beat very fine.

## To boil the Rice

Put two quarts of water to a pint of rice, let it boil till you think it is done enough, then throw in a spoonful of salt and turn it out into a cullender; then let it stand about five minutes before the fire to dry, and serve it up in a dish by itself. Dish it up and send it to table; the rice in a dish by itself.

### To ragoo a Leg of Mutton

Take all the skin and fat off, cut it very thin the right way of the grain, then butter your stew-pan, and shake some flour into it; slice half a lemon and half an onion, cut them very small, a little bundle of sweet herbs, and a blade of mace. Put all together with your meat into the pan, stir it a minute or two, and then put in six spoonfuls of gravy, and have ready an anchovy minced small; mix it with some butter and flour, stir it all together for six minutes, and then dish it up.

### To ragoo Hogs' Feet and Ears

Take your ears out of the pickle they are soused in, or boil them till they are tender, then cut them into little thin bits, about two inches long, and about as thick as a quill; put them into your stew-pan with half a pint of good gravy, or as much as will cover them, a glass of white wine, a good deal of mustard, a good piece of butter rolled in flour, and a little pepper and salt; stir all together till it is of a fine thickness, and then dish it up. The hogs' feet must not be stewed but boiled tender, then slit them in two, and put the yolk of an egg over and crumbs of bread, and broil or fry them; put the ragoo of ears in the middle, and the feet round it.

*N. B.* They make a very pretty dish fried with butter and mustard, and a little good gravy, if you like it. Then only cut the feet and ears in two. You may add half an onion, cut small.

## A rolled Rump of Beef

Cut the meat all off the bone whole, slit the inside down from top to bottom, but not through the skin, spread it open; take the flesh of two fowls and beef-suet, an equal quantity, and as much cold boiled ham (if you have it), a little pepper, an anchovy, a nutmeg grated, a little thyme, a good deal of parsley, a few mushrooms, and chop them all together, beat them in a mortar, with a half-pint basin full of crumbs of bread; mix all these together, with four yolks of eggs, lay it into the meat, cover it up, and roll it round, stick one skewer in, and tie it with a packthread cross and cross to hold it together; take a pot or large sauce-pan that will just hold it, lay a layer of bacon and a layer of beef cut in thin slices, a piece of carrot, some whole pepper, mace, sweet herbs, and a large onion; lay the rolled beef on it; just water enough to cover the top of the beef; cover it close, and let it stew very softly on a slow fire for eight or ten hours, but not too fast. When you find the beef tender, which you will know by running a skewer into the meat, then take it up, cover it up hot, boil the gravy till it is good, then strain it off, and add some mushrooms chopped, some truffles and morels cut small, two spoonfuls of red or white wine, the yolks of two eggs, and a piece of butter rolled in flour; boil it together, set the meat before the fire, baste it with butter, and throw crumbs of bread all over it; when the sauce is enough, lay the meat into the dish, and pour the sauce over it. Take care the eggs do not curdle; or you may omit the eggs.

## Sweetbreads en Cordonnier

Take three sweetbreads and parboil them, take a stew-pan and lay layers of bacon or ham and veal, over that lay the sweetbreads on with the upper side downwards, put a layer of veal and bacon over them, a pint of veal broth, three or four blades of mace, stew them gently three quarters of an hour; take the sweetbreads out, strain off the gravy through a sieve, and skim off the fat; make an omlet of yolks of eggs in the following manner: beat up four yolks of eggs, put two in a plate, and put them over a stew pan of water boiling on the fire, put another plate over them, and they will soon be done; put a little spinage juice into the other half and serve it the same; cut it out in sprigs or what form you please, and put it over the sweetbreads in the dish, and keep them as hot as you can; put some butter rolled in flour to thicken the gravy, two yolks of eggs beat up in a gill of cream; put it over the fire and keep stirring it one way till it is thick and smooth; put it under the sweetbreads and send them up. Garnish with lemon and beet-root.

## Calf's Chitterlings, or Andouilles

Take some of the largest calf's nuts, cleanse them, cut them in pieces proportionable to the length of the pud-dings you design to make, and tie one end to those pieces; then take some bacon, with a calf's udder and chaldron blanched and cut into dice or slices, put them into a stew-pan and season with fine spice pounded, a bay leaf, some salt, pepper, and shalot cut small, and about half a pint of cream; toss it up, take off the pan and thicken your mixture with four or five yolks of eggs, add some crumbs of bread, then fill up your chitterlings with the stuffing; keep it warm, tie the other ends with packthread, blanch and boil them like hog's chitterlings, let them grow cold in their own liquor before you serve them up; broil them over a moderate fire, and serve them up pretty hot. This sort of andouilles or puddings must be made in summer, when hogs are seldom killed.

## To dress Calf's Chitterlings curiously

Cut a calf's nut in slices of its length, and the thickness of a finger, together with some ham, bacon, and the white of chickens cut after the same manner; put the whole into a stew-pan seasoned with salt, pepper, sweet herbs, and spice; then take the guts cleansed, cut and divide them in parcels, and fill them with your slices; then lay in the bottom of a kettle or pan some slices of bacon and veal, season them with some pepper, salt, a bay-leaf, and an onion, and lay some bacon and veal over them; then put in a pint of white wine, and let it stew softly, close covered, with fire over and under it, if the pot or pan will allow it; then broil the puddings on a sheet of white paper, well buttered on the inside.

## To barbecue a Leg of Pork

Lay down your leg to a good fire, put into the dripping-pan two bottles of red wine, baste your pork with it all the time it is roasting; when it is enough, take up what is left in the pan, put to it two anchovies, the yolks of three eggs boiled hard and pounded fine, with a quarter of a pound of butter and half a lemon, a bunch of sweet herbs, a tea-spoonful of lemon-pickle, a spoonful of catchup, and one of tarragon vinegar, or a little tarragon shred small, boil them a few minutes, then draw your pork, and cut the skin down from the bottom of the shank in rows an inch broad, raise every other row, and roll it to the shank, strain your sauce, and pour it on boiling hot; lay oyster-patties all round the pork, and sprigs of green parsley.

## To stew Giblets

Let them be nicely scalded and picked, cut the pinions in two; cut the head, and the neck, and legs in two, and the gizzards in four; wash them very clean, put them into a stew-pan or soup pot, with three pounds of scrag of veal, just cover them with water; let them boil up, take all the scum clean off; then put three onions, two turnips, one carrot, a little thyme and parsley, stew them till they are tender, strain them through a sieve, wash the giblets clean with some warm water out of the herbs, &c.; then take a piece of butter as big as a large walnut, put it in a stew-pan, melt it, and put in a large spoonful of flour, keep it stirring till it is smooth; then put in your broth and giblets, stew them for a quarter of an hour; season with salt; or, you may add a gill of Lisbon, and just before you serve them up, chop a handful of green parsley and put in; give them a boil up, and serve them in a tureen or soup dish.

*N. B.* Three pair will make a handsome tureen-ful.

## Pigeons au Poire

Cut the feet quite off, stuff them in the shape of a pear, roll
them in the yolk of an egg and then in crumbs of bread,
stick the leg at the top, and butter a dish to lay them in;
then send them to an oven to bake, but do not let them
touch each other; when they are enough, lay them in a
dish, and pour in good gravy thickened with the yolk of an
egg, or butter rolled in flour; do not pour your gravy over
the pigeons. You may garnish with lemon. It is a pretty
genteel dish: or, for change, lay one pigeon in the middle,
the rest round, and stewed spinage between; poached eggs
on the spinage. Garnish with notched lemon and orange
cut into quarters, and have melted butter in boats.

Or thus: bone your pigeons, and stuff them with
force-meat; make them in the shape of a pear, with one
foot stuck at the small end to appear like the stalk of a
pear; rub them over with the yolk of an egg, and strew
some crumbs of bread on; fry them in a pan of good
dripping a nice light brown; put them in a drainer to
drain all the fat off; then put them in a stew-pan with a
pint of gravy, a gill of white-wine, an onion stuck with
cloves; cover them close and stew them for half an hour;
take them out, skim off all the fat, and take out the onion;
put in some butter rolled in flour, a spoonful of catchup,
the same of browning, some truffles and morels, pickled
mushrooms, two artichoke-bottoms cut in fix pieces
each, a little salt and Cayenne pepper, the juice of half a
lemon; stew it five minutes, put in your pigeons and
make them hot; put them in your dish and pour the
sauce over them. Garnish with fried force-meat balls, or
with a lemon cut in quarters.

## To bake Carp

Scale, wash, and clean a brace of carp very well; take an earthen pan deep enough to lie closely in, butter the pan a little, lay in your carp; season with mace, clove, nutmeg, and black and white pepper, a bundle of sweet herbs, an onion, and anchovy; pour in a bottle of white wine, cover it close and let them bake an hour in a hot oven, if large; if small, a less time will do them; when they are enough, carefully take them up and lay them in a dish; set it over hot water to keep it hot, and cover it close, then pour all the liquor they were baked in into a sauce-pan; let it boil a minute or two, then strain it and add half a pound of butter rolled in flour; let it boil, keep stirring it, squeeze in the juice of half a lemon and put in what salt you want; pour the sauce over the fish, lay the roes round, and garnish with lemon. Observe to skim all the fat off the liquor.

## To fry Lampreys

Bleed them and save the blood, then wash them in hot water to take off the slime, and cut them to pieces; fry them in a little fresh butter not quite enough, pour out the fat, put in a little white wine, give the pan a shake round, season it with whole pepper, nutmeg, salt, sweet herbs, and a bay-leaf, put in a few capers, a good piece of butter rolled up in flour, and the blood; give the pan a shake round often, and cover them close; when you think they are enough take them out, strain the sauce, then give them a boil quick, squeeze in a little lemon and pour over the fish. Garnish with lemon; and dress them just what way you fancy.

## To pitchcock Eels

Take a large eel and scour it well with salt to clean off all the slime; then slit it down the back, take out the bone, and cut it in three or four pieces; take the yolk of an egg and put over the inside, sprinkle crumbs of bread, with some sweet herbs and parsley chopped very fine, a little nutmeg grated, and some pepper and salt, mixed all together; then put it on a grid-iron over a clear fire, broil it of a fine light brown, dish it up, and garnish with raw parsley and horse radish; or put a boiled eel in the middle and the pitchcocked round. Garnish as above with anchovy-sauce, and parsley and butter in a boat.

## To broil Haddocks, when they are in high Season

Scale them, gut and wash them clean; do not rip open their bellies, but take the guts out with the gills; dry them in a clean cloth very well: if there be any roe or liver take it out, but put it in again; flour them well, and have a clear good fire: let your gridiron be hot and clean, lay them on, turn them quick two or three times for fear of sticking; then let one side be enough, and turn the other side: when that is done, lay them in a dish, and have plain butter in a cup, or anchovy and butter.

They eat finely salted a day or two before you dress them, and hung up to dry, or boiled with egg-sauce. Newcastle is a famous place for salted haddocks: they come in barrels, and keep a great while. Or you may make a stuffing the same as for the pike, and broil them.

# V: Everlasting Syllabub and Other Desserts

### To make Everlasting Syllabub

Take five half pints of thick cream, half a pint of Rhenish wine, half a pint of sack, and the juice of two large Seville oranges grate in just the yellow rind of three lemons, and a pound of double-refined sugar well beat and sifted; mix all together with a spoonful of orange-flower water; beat it well together with a whisk half an hour, then with a spoon take it off, and lay it on a sieve to drain, then fill your glasses: these will keep above a week, and are better made the day before. The best way to whip syllabub is, have a fine large chocolate-mill, which you must keep on purpose, and a large deep bowl to mill them in: it is both quicker done, and the froth stronger; for the thin that is left at the bottom, have ready some calf's-foot jelly boiled and clarified, there must be nothing but the calf's-foot boiled to a hard jelly; when cold take off the fat, clear it with the whites of eggs, run it through a flannel bag, and mix it with the clear which you saved of the syllabubs; sweeten it to your palate, and give it a boil, then pour it into basins, or what you please: when cold, turn it out, and it is a fine summery.

### To make Solid Syllabubs

To a quart of rich cream put a pint of white-wine, the juice of two lemons, the rind of one grated, sweeten it to your taste; mill it with a chocolate-mill till it is all of a thickness; then put it in glasses, or a bowl, and set it in a cool place till next day.

## To make a Syllabub from the Cow

Make your syllabub of either cyder or wine, sweeten it pretty sweet, and grate nutmeg in; then milk the milk into the liquor: when this is done, pour over the top half a pint or a pint of cream, according to the quantity of syllabub you make. You may make this syllabub at home, only have new milk; make it as hot as milk from the cow, and out of a teapot, or any such thing, pour it in, holding your hand very high, and strew over some currants well washed and picked, and plumped before the fire.

## To make a Trifle

Cover the bottom of your dish or bowl with Naples biscuits broke in pieces, mackeroons broke in halves, and ratafia cakes; just wet them all through with sack, then make a good boiled custard, not too thick, and when cold pour it over it, then put a syllabub over that. You may garnish it with ratina cakes, currant jelly, and flowers, and strew different coloured nonpareils over it.

*N. B.* – These are bought at the confectioners.

## To make Hartshorn Jelly

Boil half a pound of hartshorn in three quarts of water over a gentle fire, till it becomes a jelly. If you take out a little to cool, and it hangs on the spoon, it is enough. Strain it while it is hot, put it in a well-tinned sauce-pan, put to it a pint of Rhenish wine, and a quarter of a pound of loaf-sugar; beat the whites of four eggs or more to a froth; stir it all together that the whites mix well with the jelly, and pour it in, as if you were cooling it. Let it boil two or three minutes; then put in the juice of three or four lemons; let it boil a minute or two longer; when it is finely curdled, and a pure white colour, have ready a swan-skin jelly-bag over a china basin, pour in your jelly, and pour it back again till it is as clear as rock water; then set a very clean china basin under, have your glasses as clean as possible, and with a clean spoon fill your glasses. Have ready some thin rind of the lemons, and when you have filled half your glasses, throw your peel into the basin; and when the jelly is all run out of the bag, with a clean spoon, fill the rest of the glasses, and they will look of a fine amber colour. Now in putting in the ingredients there is no certain rule. You must put in lemon and sugar to your palate; most people love them sweet; and indeed they are good for nothing unless they are.

### To make a rich Cake

Take four pounds of flour dried and fisted, seven pounds of currants washed and rubbed, six pounds of the best fresh butter, two pounds of Jordan almonds blanched, and beaten with orange-flower water and sack till fine; then take four pounds of eggs, put half the whites away, three pounds of double-refined sugar beaten and fisted, a quarter of an ounce of mace, the same of cloves and cinnamon, three large nutmegs, all beaten fine, a little ginger, half a pint of sack, half a pint of right French brandy, sweet-meats to your liking, they must be orange, lemon, and citron; work your butter to a cream with your hands before any of your ingredients are in; then put in your sugar, and mix all well together; let your eggs be well beat and strained through a sieve, work in your almonds first, then put in your eggs, beat them together till they look white and thick; then put in your sack, brandy, and spices, shake your flour in by degrees, and when your oven is ready, put in your currants and sweet-meats as you put it in your hoop: it will take four hours baking in a quick oven: you must keep it beating with your hand all the while you are mixing of it, and when your currants are well washed and cleaned, let them be kept before the fire, so that they may go warm into your cake. This quantity will bake best in two hoops.

## To ice a great Cake

Take the whites of twenty-four eggs, and a pound of double-refined sugar beat and fisted fine; mix both together in a deep earthen pan, and with a whisk whisk it well for two or three hours, till it looks white and thick; then with a thin broad board, or bunch of feathers, spread it all over the top and sides of the cake; set it at a proper distance before a good clear fire, and keep turning it continually for fear of its changing colour; but a cool oven is best, and an hour will harden it: you may perfume the icing with what perfume you please.

## To make a Pound Cake

Take a pound of butter, beat it in an earthen pan with your hand one way till it is like a fine thick cream; then have ready twelve eggs, but half the whites, beat them well, and beat them up with the butter, a pound of flour beat in it, a pound of sugar, and a few carraways; beat all well together for an hour with your hand, or a great wooden spoon, butter a pan and put it in, and then bake it an hour in a quick oven.

For change, you may put in a pound of currants, clean washed and picked.

### To make a Butter Cake

You must take a dish of butter, and beat it like cream with your hands, two pounds of fine sugar well beat, three pounds of flour well dried, and mix them in with the butter, twenty-four eggs, leave out half the whites, and then beat all together for an hour: just as you are going to put it into the oven, put in a quarter of an ounce of mace, a nutmeg beat, a little sack or brandy, and seeds or currants, just as you please.

### To make a rich Seed Cake called the Nun's Cake

You must take four pounds of the finest flour, and three pounds of double-refined sugar beaten and fisted; mix them together, and dry them by the fire till you prepare the other materials; take four pounds of butter, beat it with your hand till it is soft like cream; then beat thirty-five eggs, leave out sixteen whites, strain off your eggs from the treads, and beat them and the butter together till all appears like butter; put in four or five spoonfuls of rose or orange-flower water, and beat again; then take your flour and sugar, with six ounces of carraway-seeds, and strew them in by degrees, beating it up all the time for two hours together; you may put in as much tincture of cinnamon or ambergris as you please; butter your hoop, and let it stand three hours in a moderate oven. You must observe always, in beating of butter, to do it with a cool hand, and beat it always one way in a deep earthen dish.

## To make Pepper Cakes

Take half a gill of sack, half a quarter of an ounce of whole white pepper, put it in, and boil it together a quarter of an hour; then take the pepper out, and put in as much double-refined sugar as will make it like a paste; then drop it in what shape you please on plates, and let it dry itself.

## To make Portugal Cakes

Mix into a pound of fine flour a pound of loaf-sugar beat and fisted, then rub it into a pound of pure sweet butter till it is thick like grated white bread, then put to it two spoonfuls of rose-water, two of sack, ten eggs, whip them very well with a whisk, then mix it into eight ounces of currants, mixed all well together; butter the tin pans, fill them but half full, and bake them; if made without currants they will keep half a year; add a pound of almonds blanched, and beat with rose-water as above, and leave out the flour: these are another sort, and better.

## To make a pretty Cake

Take five pounds of flour well dried, one pound of sugar, half an ounce of mace, as much nutmeg; beat your spice very fine, mix the sugar and spice in the flour, take twenty-two eggs, leave out six whites, beat them, put a pint of ale-yeast and the eggs in the flour, take two pounds and a half of fresh butter, a pint and a half of cream; set the cream and butter over the fire till the butter is melted; let it stand till it is blood-warm: before you put it into the flour, set it an hour by the fire to rise; then put in seven pounds of currants, which must be plumped in half a pint of brandy, and three quarters of a pound of candied peels: it must be an hour and a quarter in the oven: you must put two pounds of chopped raisins in the flour, and a quarter of a pint of sack: when you put the currants in, bake it in a hoop.

## To make Gingerbread

Take three quarts of fine flour, two ounces of beaten ginger, a quarter of an ounce of nutmeg, cloves, and mace beat fine, but most of the last; mix all together, three quarters of a pound of fine sugar, two pounds of treacle, set it over the fire, but do not let it boil; three quarters of a pound of butter melted in the treacle, and some candied lemon and orange peel cut fine; mix all these together well: an hour will bake it in a quick oven.

## To make little fine Cakes

One pound of butter beaten to cream, a pound and a quarter of flour, a pound of fine sugar beat fine, a pound of currants clean washed and picked, six eggs, two whites left out, beat them fine; mix the flour, sugar, and eggs by degrees into the batter, beat it all well with both hands; either make into little cakes, or bake it in one.

## Another Sort of little Cakes

A pound of flour, and half a pound of sugar; beat half a pound of butter with your hand, and mix them well together: bake it in little cakes.

## To make Drop-Biscuits

Take eight eggs, and one pound of double-refined sugar beaten fine, twelve ounces of fine flour well dried, beat your eggs very well, then put in your sugar and beat it, and then your flour by degrees, beat it all very well together without ceasing; your oven must be as hot as for halfpenny bread; then flour some sheets of tin, and drop your biscuits of what bigness you please, put them in the oven as fast as you can, and when you see them rise, watch them; if they begin to colour, take them out, and put in more; and if the first is not enough, put them in again: if they are right done, they will have a white ice on them: you may, if you choose, put in a few carraways; when they are all baked, put them in the oven again to dry, then keep them in a very dry place.

## To make common Biscuits

Beat up six eggs, with a spoonful of rose-water and a spoonful of sack; then add a pound of fine powdered sugar, and a pound of flour; mix them into the eggs by degrees, and an ounce of coriander-seeds; mix all well together, shape them on white thin paper, or tin moulds, in any form you please: beat the white of an egg, with a feather rub them over, and dust fine sugar over them; set them in an oven moderately heated, till they rise and come to a good colour, take them out; and when you have done with the oven, if you have no stove to dry them in, put them in the oven again, and let them stand all night to dry.

## To make French Biscuits

Having a pair of clean scales ready, in one scale put three new-laid eggs, in the other scale put as much dried flour, an equal weight with the eggs, take out the flour, and put in as much fine powdered sugar; first beat the whites of the eggs up well with a whisk till they are of a fine froth; then whip in half an ounce of candied lemon-peel cut very thin and fine, and beat well: then by degrees whip in the flour and sugar, then slip in the yolks, and with a spoon temper it well together; then shape your biscuits on fine white paper with your spoon, and throw powdered sugar over them: bake them in a moderate oven, not too hot, giving them a fine colour on the top: when they are baked, with a fine knife cut them off from the paper, and lay them in boxes for use.

## To make Mackeroons

Take a pound of almonds, let them be scalded, blanched, and thrown into cold water, then dry them in a cloth, and pound them in a mortar, moisten them with orange-flower water, or the white of an egg, lest they turn to oil; afterwards take an equal quantity of fine powder sugar, with three or four whites of eggs, and a little musk, beat all well together, and shape them on a wafer-paper, with a spoon round: bake them in a gentle oven on tin plates.

## To make Shrewsbury Cakes

Take two pounds of flour, a pound of sugar finely fearced, mix them together (take out a quarter of a pound to roll them in); take four eggs beat, four spoonfuls of cream, and two spoonfuls of rose-water; beat them well together, and mix them with the flour into a paste, roll them into thin cakes, and bake them in a quick oven.

## To make Madling Cakes

To a quarter of a peck of flour, well dried at the fire, add two pounds of mutton-suet dried and strained clear off; when it is a little cool, mix it well with the flour, some salt, and a very little all-spice beat fine; take half a pint of good yeast, and put in half a pint of water, stir it well together, strain it, and mix up your flour into a paste of moderate stiffness: you must add as much cold water as will make the paste of a right order; make it into cakes about the thickness and bigness of an oat-cake: have ready some currants clean washed and picked, strew some just in the middle of your cakes between your dough, so that none can be seen till the cake is broke. You may leave the currants out, if you do not choose them.

## Wiggs

Take three pounds of well dried flour, one nutmeg, a little mace and salt, and almost half a pound of carraway-comfits; mix these well together, and melt half a pound of butter in a pint of sweet thick cream, six spoonfuls of good sack, four yolks and three whites of eggs, and near a pint of good light yeast; work these well together, cover it, and set it down to the fire to rise; then let them rest, and lay the remainder, the half pound of carraways on the top of the wiggs, and put them upon papers well floured and dried, and let them have as quick an oven as for tarts.

## To make Buns

Take two pounds of fine flour, a pint of good ale-yeast, put a little sack in the yeast, and three eggs beaten, knead all these together with a little warm milk, a little nutmeg, and a little salt; and lay it before the fire till it rises very light, then knead in a pound of fresh butter, a pound of rough carraway-comfits, and bake them in a quick oven, in what shape you please, on floured paper.

## A Cake the Spanish Way

Take twelve eggs, three quarters of a pound of the best moist sugar, mill them in a chocolate-mill till they are all of a lather; then mix in one pound of flour, half a pound of pounded almonds, two ounces of candied orange-peel, two ounces of citron, four large spoonfuls of orange-water, half an ounce of cinnamon, and a glass of sack: it is better when baked in a slow oven.

## How to make Uxbridge Cakes

Take a pound of wheat-flour, seven pounds of currants, half a nutmeg, four pounds of butter, rub your butter cold very well amongst the meal; dress your currants very well in the flour, butter, and seasoning; and knead it with so much good new yeast as will make it into a pretty high paste, (usually two pennyworth of yeast to that quantity); after it is kneaded well together let it stand an hour to rise: you may put half a pound of paste in a cake.

## To make Carraway Cakes

Take two pounds of white flour, and two pounds of coarse loaf-sugar well dried and fine fisted; after the flour and sugar are fisted and weighed, mingle them together, fist the flour and sugar together, through a hair sieve, into the bowl you use it in; to them you must have two pounds of good butter, eighteen eggs, leaving out eight of the whites; to these you must add four ounces of candied orange, five or six ounces of carraway-comfits; you must first work the butter with rose-water till you can see none of the water, and your butter must be very soft; then put in flour and sugar, a little at a time, and likewise your eggs; but you must beat your eggs very well, with ten spoonfuls of sack, so you must put in each as you think fit, keeping it constantly beating with your hand till you have put it into the hoop for the oven; do not put in your sweet-meats and seeds till you are ready to put it into your hoops; you must have three or four doubles of cap-paper under the cakes, and butter the paper and hoop: you must sift some fine sugar upon your cake when it goes into the oven.

## To make a Bride Cake

Take four pounds of fine flour well dried, four pounds of fresh butter, two pounds of loaf-sugar, pound and sift fine a quarter of an ounce of mace, the same of nutmegs, to every pound of flour put eight eggs, wash four pounds of currants, pick them well, and dry them before the fire, blanch a pound of sweet almonds, and cut them length-ways very thin, a pound of citron, one pound of candied orange, the same of candied lemon, half a pint of brandy; first work the butter with your hand to a cream, then beat in your sugar a quarter of an hour, beat the whites of your eggs to a very strong froth, mix them with your sugar and butter, beat your yolks half an hour at least, and mix them with your cake, then put in your flour, mace, and nutmeg, keep beating it well till your oven is ready, put in your brandy, and beat your currants and almonds lightly in, tie three sheets of paper round the bottom of your hoop to keep it from running out, rub it well with butter, put in your cake, and lay your sweet meats in three lays, with cake betwixt every lay; after it is risen and coloured, cover it with paper before your oven is stopped up: it will take three hours baking.

# VI: Bread-baking and Cheese-making

### To make White Bread, after the London Way

Take a bushel of the finest flour well dressed, put it in the kneading-trough at one end, take a gallon of water (which we call liquor) and some yeast; stir it into the liquor till it looks of a good brown colour and begins to curdle, strain and mix it with your flour till it is about the thickness of a seed-cake; then cover it with the lid of the trough, and let it stand three hours; and as soon as you see it begin to fall, take a gallon more of liquor; weigh three quarters of a pound of salt, and with your hand mix it well with the water: strain it, and with this liquor make your dough of a moderate thickness, fit to make up into loaves; then cover it again with the lid, and let it stand three hours more. In the mean time, put the wood into the oven and heat it. It will take two hours heating. When your spunge has stood its proper time, clear the oven, and begin to make your bread. Set it in the oven, and close it up, and three hours will bake it. When once it is in, you must not open the oven till the bread is baked; and observe in summer that your water be milk-warm, and in winter as hot as you can bear your finger in it.

*N. B.* As to the quantity of liquor your dough will take, experience will teach you in two or three times making; for all flour does not want the same quantity of liquor; and if you make any quantity, it will raise up the lid and run over.

## To make French Bread

Take three quarts of water, and one of milk; in winter scalding hot, in summer a little more than milk warm; season it well with salt, then take a pint and a half of good ale yeast not bitter, lay it in a gallon of water the night before, pour it off the water, stir in your yeast into the milk and water, then with your hand break in a little more than a quarter of a pound of butter, work it well till it is dissolved, then beat up two eggs in a basin, and stir them in; have about a peck and a half of flour, mix it with your liquor; in winter make your dough pretty stiff, in summer more slack: so that you may use a little more or less flour, according to the stiffness of your dough: mix it well, but the less you work the better: make it into rolls, and have a very quick oven. When they have lain about a quarter of an hour, turn them on the other side, let them lie about a quarter longer, and then take them out and chip all your French bread with a knife, which is better than rasping it, and make it look spungy and of a fine yellow, whereas the rasping takes off all that fine colour, and makes it look too smooth. You must stir your liquor into the flour as you do for the pie-crust. After your dough is made, cover it with a cloth, and let it lie to rise while the oven is heating.

## To make Muffins and Oat-Cakes

To a bushel of Hertfordshire white flour, take a pint and a half of good ale yeast, from pale malt, if you can get it, because it is whitest; let the yeast lie in water all night, the next day pour off the water clear, make two gallons of water just milk-warm, not to scald your yeast, and two ounces of salt; mix your water, yeast, and salt well together for about a quarter of an hour; then strain it and mix up your dough as light as possible; and let it lie in your trough an hour to rise; then with your hand roll it, and pull it into little pieces about as big as a large walnut, roll them with your hand like a ball, lay them on your table, and as fast as you do them, lay a piece of flannel over them, and be sure to keep your dough covered with flannel; when you have rolled out all your dough, begin to bake the first, and by that time they will be spread out in the right form; lay them on your iron; as one side begins to change colour, turn the other; take great care they do not burn, or be too much discoloured, but that you will be a judge of in two or three makings. Take care the middle of the iron is not too hot, as it will be; but then you may put a brick-bat or two in the middle of the fire to slacken the heat. The thing you bake on must be made thus:

Build a place as if you were going to set a copper; and, in the stead of a copper, a piece of iron all over the top, fixed in form just the same as the bottom of an iron pot, and make your fire underneath with coal, as in a copper. Observe, muffins are made the same way; only this, when you pull them to pieces, roll them in a good deal of flour, and with a rolling-pin roll them thin, cover them with a piece of flannel, and they will rise to a proper thickness; and if you find them too big or too little, you must roll dough accordingly. These must not be the least discoloured. When you eat them, toast them crisp on both sides, then with your hand pull them open, and they will be like a honeycomb; lay in as much butter as you intend to use, then clap them together again, and set it by the fire. When you think the butter is melted, turn them, that both sides may be buttered alike, but do not touch them with a knife, either to spread, or cut them open; if you do, they will be as heavy as lead, only when they are buttered and done, you may cut them across with a knife.

N. B. Some flour will soak up a quart or three pints more water than other flour; then you must add more water, or shake in more flour in making up, for the dough must be as light as possible.

## A Method to preserve a large Stock of Yeast, which will keep and be of Use for several Months, either to make Bread or Cakes

When you have yeast in plenty, take a quantity of it, stir and work it well with a whisk until it becomes liquid and thin, then get a large wooden platter, cooler, or tub, clean and dry, and with a soft brush lay a thin layer of the yeast on the tub, and turn the mouth downwards that no dust may fall upon it, but so that the air may get under to dry it; when that coat is very dry, then lay on another till you have a sufficient quantity, even two or three inches thick, to serve for several months, always taking care the yeast in the tub be very dry before you lay more on: when you have occasion to use this yeast, cut a piece off and lay it in warm water; stir it together, and it will be fit for use. If it is for brewing, take a large handful of birch tied together, and dip it into the yeast and hang it up to dry; take great care no dust comes to it, and so you may do as many as you please. When your beer is fit to set to work, throw in one of these, and it will make it work as well as if you had fresh yeast.

You must whip it about in the wort, and then let it lie; when the vat works well, take out the broom and dry it again, and it will do for the next brewing.

*N.B.* In the building of your oven for baking, observe that you make it round, low roofed, and a little mouth; then it will take less fire, and keep in the heat better than a long oven and high roofed, and will bake the bread better.

## To make Slip-coat Cheese

Take six quarts of new milk hot from the cow, the stroakings, and put to it two spoonfuls of rennet; and when it is hard coming, lay it into the fat with a spoon, not breaking it all; then press it with a four-pound weight, turning of it with a dry cloth once an hour, and every day shifting it into fresh grass. It will be ready to cut, if the weather be hot, in fourteen days.

## To make a Brick-Bat Cheese.
### It must be made in September

Take two gallons of new milk, and a quart of good cream, heat the cream, put in two spoonfuls of rennet, and when it is come, break it a little, then put it into a wooden mould, in the shape of a brick. It must be half a year old before you eat it: you must press it a little, and so dry it.

## To make Cream Cheese

Put one large spoonful of steep to five quarts of afterings, break it down light, put it upon a cloth in a sieve bottom, and let it run till dry, break it, cut and turn it in a clean cloth, then put it into the sieve again, and put on it a two-pound weight, sprinkle a little salt on it and let it stand all night, then lay it on a board to dry; when dry, lay a few strawberry leaves on it, and ripen it between two pewter dishes in a warm place, turn it, and put on fresh leaves every day.

## To make Bullace Cheese

Take your bullace when they are full ripe, put them into a pot, and to every quart of bullace put a quarter of a pound of loaf-sugar beat small; bake them in a moderate oven till they are soft, then rub them through a hair sieve; to every pound of pulp add half a pound of loaf-sugar beat fine, then boil it an hour and a half over a slow fire, and keep stirring it all the time, then pour it into potting pots, and tie brandy papers over them, and keep them in a dry place; when it has stood a few months, it will cut out very bright and fine.

*N. B.* You may make sloe cheese the same way.

## To make Stilton Cheese

Take the night's cream and put it to the morning's new milk with the rennet, when the curd is come, it is not to be broken, as is done with other cheeses, but take it out with a soil-dish all together, and place it on a sieve to drain gradually, and as it drains, keep gradually pressing it till it becomes firm and dry, then place it in a wooden hoop; afterwards to be kept dry on boards, turned frequently, with cloth binders round it, which are to be tightened as occasion requires. In some dairies the cheeses, after being taken out of the wooden hoop, are bound tight round with a cloth, which is changed every day till the cheese is firm enough to support itself; after the cloth is taken off they are rubbed all over daily with a brush for two or three months, and if the weather is damp, twice a day; and even before the cloth is taken off, the top and bottom are well rubbed every day.

*N. B.* The dairy-maid must not be disheartened if she does not perfectly succeed the first time.

# VII: Pressing and Brewing

### The best Way to make Raisin Wine

Take a clean wine or brandy hogshead, take great care it is very sweet and clean, put in two hundred of raisins (stalks and all), and then fill the vessel with fine clear spring-water; let it stand till you think it has done hissing, then throw in two quarts of fine French brandy; put in the bung slightly, and, in about three weeks or a month (if you are sure it has done fretting), stop it down close; let it stand six months, peg it near the top, and if you find it very fine and good, fit for drinking, bottle it off, or else stop it up again, and let it stand six months longer: it should stand six months in the bottle. This is by much the best way of making it, as I have seen by experience, as the wine will be much stronger, but less of it: the different sorts of raisins make quite a different wine; and after you have drawn off all the wine, throw on ten gallons of spring-water; take off the head of the barrel and stir it well twice a day, pressing the raisins as well as you can; let it stand a fortnight or three weeks, then draw it off into a proper vessel to hold it, and squeeze the raisins well; add two quarts of brandy, and two quarts of syrup of alder-berries, stop it close when it has done working, and in about three months it will be fit for drinking. If you do not choose to make this wine, fill your hogshead with spring-water, and set it in the sun for three or four months, and it will make excellent vinegar.

## How to make Blackberry Wine

Take your berries when full ripe, put them into a large vessel of wood or stone, with a spicket in it, and pour upon them as much boiling water as will just appear at the top of them; as soon as you can endure your hand in them, bruise them very well, till all the berries be broke: then let them stand close covered till the berries be well wrought up to the top, which usually is three or four days, then draw off the clear juice into another vessel; and add to every ten quarts of this liquor one pound of sugar, stir it well in, and let it stand to work in another vessel like the first, a week or ten days; then draw it off at the spicket through a jelly-bag into a large vessel; take four ounces of isinglass, lay it in steep twelve hours in a pint of white wine; the next morning boil it till it be all dissolved upon a slow fire; then take a gallon of your blackberry-juice, put in the dissolved isinglass, give it a boil together, and put it in hot.

## To make Alder Wine

Pick the alder-berries when full ripe, put them into a stone-jar and set them in the oven, or a kettle of boiling water till the jar is hot through; then take them out and strain them through a coarse cloth, wringing the berries, and put the juice into a clean kettle: to every quart of juice put a pound of fine Lisbon sugar, let it boil, and skim it well; when it is clear and fine, pour it into a jar; when cold, cover it close, and keep it till you make raisin wine; then when you tun your wine, to every gallon of wine put half a pint of the elder-syrup.

## To make Orange Wine

Take twelve pounds of the best powder sugar, with the whites of eight or ten eggs well beaten, into six gallons of spring-water, and boil three quarters of an hour; when cold, put into it six spoonfuls of yeast, and the juice of twelve lemons, which, being pared, must stand with two pounds of white sugar in a tankard, and in the morning skim off the top, and then put it into the water; then add the juice and rinds of fifty oranges, but not the white parts of the rinds, and so let it work all together two days and two nights; then add two quarts of Rhenish or white wine, and put it into your vessel.

## To make Gooseberry Wine

Gather your gooseberries in dry weather, when they are half ripe, pick them, and bruise a peck in a tub, with a wooden mallet; then take a horse-hair cloth and press them as much as possible, without breaking the feeds; when you have pressed out all the juice, to every gallon of gooseberries put three pounds of fine dry powder sugar, stir it all together till the sugar is dissolved, then put it in a vessel or cask, which must be quite full: if ten or twelve gallons, let it stand a fortnight; if a twenty gallon cask, five weeks. Set it in a cool place, then draw it off from the lees, clear the vessel of the lees, and pour in the clear liquor again: if it be a ten gallon cask, let it stand three months; if a twenty gallon, four months; then bottle it off.

## To make Birch Wine

The season for procuring the liquor from the birch-trees is the beginning of March, while the sap is rising, and before the leaves shoot out; for when the sap is come forward, and the leaves appear, the juice, by being long digested in the bark, grows thick and coloured, which before was thin and clear. The method of procuring the juice is, by boring holes in the body of the tree, and putting in fossets, which are commonly made of the branches of elder, the pith being taken out. You may without hurting the tree, if large, tap it in several places, four or five at a time, and by that means save from a good many trees several gallons every day; if you have not enough in one day, the bottles in which it drops must be corked close, and rosined or waxed; however, make use of it as soon as you can. Take the sap and boil it as long as any scum rises, skimming it all the time: to every gallon of liquor put four pounds of good sugar, the thin peel of a lemon, boil it afterwards half an hour, skimming it very well, pour it into a clean tub, and when it is almost cold, set it to work with yeast spread upon a toast, let it stand five or six days, stirring it often; then take such a cask as will hold the liquor, fire a large match dipped in brimstone, and throw it into the cask, stop it close till the match is extinguished, tun your wine, lay the bung on light till you find it has done working; stop it close and keep it three months, then bottle it off.

## To make Quince Wine

Gather the quinces when dry and full ripe; take twenty large quinces, wipe them clean with a coarse cloth, and grate them with a large grate or rasp as near the core as you can, but none of the core; boil a gallon of spring-water, throw in your quinces, let it boil softly about a quarter of an hour; then strain them well into an earthen pan on two pounds of double-refined sugar, pare the peel of two large lemons, throw in and squeeze the juice through a sieve, stir it about till it is very cool, then toast a little bit of bread very thin and brown, rub a little yeast on it, let it stand close covered twenty-four hours, then take out the toast and lemon, put it up in a keg, keep it three months, and then bottle it. If you make a twenty gallon cask, let it stand six months before you bottle it; when you strain your quinces, you are to wring them hard in a coarse cloth.

## To make Cowslip or Clary Wine

Take six gallons of water, twelve pounds of sugar, the juice of six lemons, the whites of four eggs beat very well, put all together in a kettle, let it boil half an hour, skim it very well: take a peck of cowslips (if dry ones, half a peck), put them into a tub, with the thin peeling of six lemons, then pour on the boiling liquor, and stir them about; when almost cold, put in a thin toast baked dry and rubbed with yeast: let it stand two or three days to work. If you put in (before you tun it) six ounces of syrup of citron or lemons, with a quart of Rhenish wine, it will be a great addition; the third day strain it off, and squeeze the cowslips through a coarse cloth; then strain it through a flannel bag, and tun it up; lay the bung loose for two or three days to see if it works, and if it does not, bung it down tight; let it stand three months, then bottle it.

## To make Turnip Wine

Take a good many turnips, pare, slice, and put them in a cyder-press, and press out all the juice very well; to every gallon of juice have three pounds of lump-sugar, have a vessel ready just big enough to hold the juice, put your sugar into a vessel, and also to every gallon of juice half a pint of brandy; pour in the juice, and lay something over the bung for a week, to see if it works; if it does, you must not bung it down till it has done working: then stop it close for three months, and draw it off in another vessel. When it is fine, bottle it off.

## How to make Mead

Take ten gallons of water, and two gallons of honey, a handful of raced ginger; then take two lemons, cut them in pieces, and put them into it, boil it very well, keep it skimming; let it stand all night in the same vessel you boil it in, the next morning barrel it up, with two or three spoonfuls of good yeast. About three weeks or a month after, you may bottle it.

## RULES FOR BREWING

Care must be taken, in the first place, to have the malt clean; and after it is ground, it ought to stand four or five days.

For strong October, five quarters of malt to three hogsheads, and twenty-four pounds of hops. This will afterwards make two hogsheads of good keeping small beer, allowing five pounds of hops to it.

For middling beer, a quarter of malt makes a hogshead

of ale, and one of small beer; or it will make three hogsheads of good small beer, allowing eight pounds of hops.
This will keep all the year. Or it will make twenty gallons
of strong ale, and two hogsheads of small beer that will
keep all the year.

If you intend your ale to keep a great while, allow a
pound of hops to every bushel; if to keep six months,
five pounds to a hogshead; if for present drinking, three
pounds to a hogshead, and the softest and clearest water
you can get.

Observe the day before to have all your vessels very
clean, and never use your tubs for any other use except
to make wines.

Let your cask be very clean the day before with boiling water; and if your bung is big enough, scrub them
well with a little birch-broom or brush; but if they be
very bad, take out the heads, and let them be scrubbed
clean with a hand-brush, sand, and fullers-earth. Put on
the head again, and scald them well, throw into the barrel a piece of unslacked lime, and stop the bung close.

The first copper of water, when it boils, pour into
your mash-tub, and let it be cool enough to see your face
in; then put in your malt, and let it be well mashed; have
a copper of water boiling in the mean time, and when
your malt is well mashed, fill your mashing-tub, stir it
well again, and cover it over with the sacks. Let it stand
three hours, set a broad shallow tub under the cock, let
it run very softly; and if it is thick, throw it up again till
it runs fine, then throw a handful of hops in the under
tub, let the mash run into it, and fill your tubs till all is
run off. Have water boiling in the copper, and lay as

much more as you have occasion for, allowing one third for boiling and waste. Let that stand an hour, boiling more water to fill the mash-tub for small beer; let the fire down a little, and put it into tubs enough to fill your mash. Let the second mash be run off, and fill your copper with the first wort; put in part of your hops, and make it boil quick. About an hour is long enough; when it has half boiled, throw in a handful of salt. Have a clean white wand, and dip it into the copper; and if the wort feels clammy, it is boiled enough; then slacken your fire, and take off your wort. Have ready a large tub, put two sticks across, and set your straining basket over the tub on the sticks, and strain your wort through it. Put other wort on to boil with the rest of the hops; let your mash be covered again with water, and thin your wort that is cooled in as many things as you can; for the thinner it lies, and the quicker it cools, the better. When quite cool, put it into the tunning-tub. Throw a handful of salt into every boil. When the mash has stood an hour, draw it off; then fill your mash with cold water, take off the wort in the copper, and order it as before. When cool, add to it the first in the tub; so soon as you empty one copper, fill the other, so boil your small beer well. Let the last mash run off, and when both are boiled with fresh hops, order them as the two first boilings; when cool, empty the mash-tub, and put the small beer to work there. When cool enough, work it; set a wooden bowl of yeast in the beer, and it will work over with a little of the beer in the boil. Stir your tun up every twelve hours, let it stand two days, then tun it, taking off the yeast. Fill your vessels full, and save some to fill your barrels; let it stand till it has done working; then lay your bung lightly for a fortnight, after that stop it as close as you can. Mind you have a vent-peg at the top of the vessel; in warm weather open it; and if your drink hisses, as it often will, loosen it till it has done, then stop it close again. If you can boil your ale in one boiling it is best, if your copper will allow of it; if not, boil it as conveniency serves.

When you come to draw your beer, and find it is not fine, draw off a gallon, and set it on the fire, with two ounces of isinglass cut small and beat; dissolve it in the beer over the fire: when it is all melted, let it stand till it is cold, and pour it in at the bung, which must lay loose on till it has done fermenting, then stop it close for a month. Take great care your casks are not musty, or have any ill taste; if they have, it is a hard thing to sweeten them. You are to wash your casks with cold water before you scald them, and they should lie a day or two soaking, and clean them well, then scald them.

### The best Thing for Rope

Mix two handfuls of bean flour and one handful of salt, throw this into a kilderkin of beer, do not stop it close till it has done fermenting, then let it stand a month, and draw it off; but sometimes nothing will do with it.

### When a Barrel of Beer has turned Sour

To a kilderkin of beer throw in at the bung a quart of oatmeal, lay the bung on loose two or three days, then stop it down close, and let it stand a month. Some throw in a piece of chalk as big as a turkey's egg, and when it has done working, stop it close for a month, then tap it.

## How to make Cyder

After all your apples are bruised, take half of your quantity and squeeze them; and the juice you press from them, pour upon the others half bruised, but not squeezed, in a tub for the purpose, having a tap at the bottom; let the juice remain upon the apples three or four days; then pull out your tap, and let your juice run into some other vessel set under the tub to receive it; and if it runs thick, as at the first it will, pour it upon the apples again, till you see it run clear; and as you have a quantity, put it into your vessel, but do not force the cyder, but let it drop as long as it will of its own accord; having done this, after you perceive that the sides begin to work, take a quantity of isinglass (an ounce will serve forty gallons), infuse this in some of the cyder till it be dissolved; put to an ounce of isinglass a quart of cyder, and when it is so dissolved, pour it into the vessel, and stop it close for two days, or something more; then draw off the cyder into another vessel: this do so often till you perceive your cyder to be free from all manner of sediment that may make it ferment and fret itself: after Christmas you may boil it. You may, by pouring water on the apples and pressing them, make a pretty small cyder: if it be thick and muddy, by using isinglass, you may make it as clear as the rest; you must dissolve the isinglass over the fire till it be jelly.

## For fining Cyder

Take two quarts of skim-milk, four ounces of isinglass, cut the isinglass in pieces, and work it lukewarm in the milk over the fire; and when it is dissolved, then put it cold into the hogshead of cyder, and take a long stick and stir it well from top to bottom for half a quarter of an hour.

## After it has fined

Take ten pounds of raisins of the sun, two ounces of turmerick, half an ounce of ginger beaten; then take a quantity of raisins, and grind them as you do mustard-seed in a bowl, with a little cyder, and so the rest of the raisins; then sprinkle the turmerick and ginger amongst it; then put all into a fine canvass bag, and hang it in the middle of the hogshead close, and let it lie. After the cyder has stood thus a fortnight or a month, then you may bottle it at your pleasure.

# VIII: Preserving and Storing

(Many of the Receipts in this Chapter are very
useful for Captains of Ships, and Families.)


### To make Catchup to keep twenty Years

Take a gallon of strong stale beer, one pound of anchovies washed from the pickle, a pound of shalots peeled,
half an ounce of mace, half an ounce of cloves, a quarter
of an ounce of whole pepper, three or four large races of
ginger, two quarts of the large mushroom-slaps rubbed
to pieces; cover all this close, and let it simmer till it is
half wasted, then strain it through a flannel bag; let it
stand till it is quite cold, then bottle it. You may carry it
to the Indies. A spoonful of this to a pound of fresh butter melted makes a fine fish-sauce, or in the room of
gravy sauce. The stronger and staler the beer is, the better the catchup will be.


### To make Fish-Sauce to keep the whole Year

You must take twenty-four anchovies, chop them, bones
and all, put to them ten shalots cut small, a handful of
scraped horse-radish, a quarter of an ounce of mace, a
quart of white wine, a pint of water, one lemon cut into
slices, half a pint of anchovy liquor, a pint of red wine,
twelve cloves, twelve pepper-corns; boil them together
till it comes to a quart; strain it off, cover it close, and

keep it in a cold dry place. Two spoonfuls will be sufficient for a pound of butter.

It is a pretty sauce either for boiled fowl, veal, &c. or in the room of gravy, lowering it with hot water, and thickening it with a piece of butter rolled in flour.

### To put Dripping to fry Fish, Meat, Fritters, &c

Take six pounds of good beef-dripping, boil it in soft water, strain it into a pan, let it stand till cold; then take off the hard fat, and scrape off the gravy which sticks to the inside; thus do eight times; when it is cold and hard, take it off clean from the water, put it into a large sauce-pan with fix bay-leaves, twelve cloves, half a pound of salt, and a quarter of a pound of whole pepper; let the fat be all melted and just hot, let it stand till it is hot enough to strain through a sieve into the pot, and stand till it is quite cold, then cover it up: thus you may do what quantity you please. The best way to keep any sort of dripping is to turn the pot upside down, and then no rats can get at it. If it will keep on ship board, it will make as fine puff-paste crust as any butter can do, or crust for puddings, &c.

### To pickle Mushrooms for the Sea

Wash them clean with a piece of flannel in salt and water, put them into a sauce-pan and throw a little salt over them; let them boil up three times in their own liquor, then throw them into a sieve to drain, and spread them on a clean cloth; let them lie till cold, then put them in wide-mouthed bottles, put in with them a good deal of whole mace, a little nutmeg sliced, and a few cloves: boil the sugar-vinegar of your own making with a good deal of whole pepper, some races of ginger, and two or three bay leaves; let it boil a few minutes, then strain it, when it is cold pour it on and fill the bottle with mutton fat fried; cork them, tie a bladder, then a leather over them, keep it down close, and in as cool a place as possible.

## To make Mushroom Powder

Take half a peck of fine large thick mushrooms, wash them clean from grit and dirt with a flannel rag, scrape out the inside, cut out all the worms, put them into a kettle over the fire without any water, two large onions stuck with cloves, a large handful of salt, a quarter of an ounce of mace, two tea-spoonfuls of beaten pepper, let them simmer till the liquor is boiled away; take great care they do not burn; then lay them on sieves to dry in the sun, or in tin plates, and set them in a slack oven all night to dry, till they will beat to powder: press the powder down hard in a pot, and keep it for use. You may put what quantity you please for the sauce.

## To keep Artichoke-Bottoms dry

Boil them just so as you can pull off the leaves and the choke, cut them from the stalks, lay them on tin plates, set them in a very cool oven, and repeat it till they are quite dry; then put them in a paper bag, tie them up close, and hang them up, and always keep them in a dry place; and when you use them lay them in warm water till they are tender; shift the water two or three times. They are fine in almost all sauces cut in little pieces, and put in just before your sauce is enough.

## To make a Gravy-Soup

Only boil soft water, and put as much of the strong soup to it as will make it to your palate; let it boil, and if it wants salt, you must season it.

## To make Peas-Soup

Get a quart of peas, boil them in two gallons of water till they are tender, then have ready a piece of salt pork, or beef, which has been laid in water the night before, put it into the pot, with two large onions pealed, a bundle of sweet herbs, celery (if you have it), half a quarter of an ounce of whole pepper; let it boil till the meat is enough, then take it up, and if the soup is not enough, let it boil till the soup is good; then strain it, set it on again to boil, and rub in a good deal of dry mint; keep the meat hot; when the soup is ready, put in the meat again for a few minutes and let it boil, then serve it away: if you add a piece of the portable soup, it will be very good.

## To make a Pudding of Pork, Beef, &c

Make a good crust with the dripping, or mutton-suet (if you have it) shred fine; make a thick crust, take a piece of salt pork or beef which has been twenty-four hours in soft water, season it with a little pepper, put it into this crust, roll it up close, tie it in cloth, and boil it; if of about four or five pounds, boil it five hours.

And when you kill mutton, make a pudding the same way, only cut the steaks thin; season them with pepper and salt, and boil it three hours, if large; or two hours, if small; and so according to the size.

Apple-pudding make with the same crust, only pare

the apples, core them, and fill your pudding; if large, it will take five hours boiling; when it is enough, lay it in the dish, cut a hole in the top and stir in butter and sugar; lay the piece on again, and send it to table.

A prune-pudding eats fine made the same way, only when the crust is ready fill it with prunes, and sweeten it according to your fancy, close it up, and boil it two hours.

## To make a Rice-Pudding

Take what rice you think proper, tie it loose in a cloth, and boil it an hour; then take it up and untie it, grate a good deal of nutmeg in, stir in a good piece of butter, and sweeten to your palate; tie it up close, boil it an hour more, then take it up and turn it into your dish; melt butter, with a little sugar, and a little white wine for sauce.

## To make a Suet-Pudding

Get a pound of suet shred fine, a pound of flour, a pound of currants picked clean, half a pound of raisins stoned, two tea spoonfuls of beaten ginger, and a spoonful of tincture of saffron; mix all together with salt water very thick; then either boil or bake it.

## A Liver-Pudding boiled

Get the liver of the sheep, when you kill one, and cut it as thin as you can, and chop it; mix it with as much suet shred fine, half as many crumbs of bread or biscuit grated, season is with some sweet herbs shred fine, a little nutmeg grated, a little beaten pepper, and an anchovy shred fine; mix all together with a little salt, or the anchovy liquor, with a piece of butter, till the crust and close it; boil it three hours.

## To make an Oatmeal-Pudding

Get a pint of oatmeal once cut, a pound of suet shred fine, a pound of currants, and half a pound of raisins stoned; mix all together well with a little salt, tie it in a cloth, leaving room for the swelling.

## To make a Peas-Pudding

Boil it till it is quite tender, then take it up, untie it, stir in a good piece of butter, a little salt, and a good deal of beaten pepper, then tie it up tight again, boil it an hour longer, and it will eat fine.

## To make a Harrico of French Beans

Take a pint of the seeds of French beans which are ready dried for sowing, wash them clean and put them into a two-quart sauce-pan, fill it with water, and let them boil two hours; if the water washes away too much, you must put in more boiling water to keep them boiling; in the meantime take almost half a pound of nice fresh butter, put it into a clean stew-pan, and when it is all melted, and done making any noise, have ready a pint basin heaped up with onions peeled and sliced thin, throw them into the pan and fry them of a fine brown, stirring them about that they may be all alike, then pour off the clear water from the beans into a basin, and throw the beans all into the stew-pan; stir all together, and throw in a large tea-spoonful of beaten pepper, two heaped full of salt, and stir it all together for two or three minutes. You may make this dish of what thickness you think proper (either to eat with a spoon or otherwise) with the liquor you poured off the beans. For change you may make it thin enough for soup. When it is of the proper thickness you like it, take it off the fire, and stir in a large spoonful of vinegar and the yolk of two eggs beat. The eggs may be left out if disliked. Dish in up and send it to table.

## To make a Fowl Pie

First make rich thick crust, cover the dish with the paste, then take some very fine bacon, or cold boiled ham, slice it, and lay a layer all over; season with a little pepper, then put in the fowl, after it is picked and cleaned, and singed; shake a very little pepper and salt into the belly, put in a little water, cover it with ham seasoned with a little beaten pepper, put on the lid and bake it two hours: when it comes out of the oven, take half a pint of water, boil it, and add to it as much of the strong soup as will make the gravy quite rich, pour it boiling hot into the pie, and lay on the lid again; send it to table hot. Or lay a piece of beef or pork in soft water twenty-four hours, slice it in the room of the ham, and it will eat fine.

## To make a Cheshire Pork Pie for Sea

Take some salt pork that has been boiled, cut it into thin slices, an equal quantity of potatoes pared and sliced thin, make a good crust, cover the dish, lay a layer of meat seasoned with a little pepper, and a layer of potatoes, then a layer of meat, a layer of potatoes, and so on till your pie is full; season it with pepper when it is full, lay some butter on the top, and fill your dish above half full of soft water; close your pie up, and bake it in a gentle oven.

## To make Sea Venison

When you kill a sheep, keep stirring the blood all the time till it is cold, or at least as cold as it will be, that it may not congeal; then cut up the sheep, take one side, cut the leg like a haunch, cut off the shoulder and loin, the neck and breast in two, steep them all in the blood as long as the weather will permit you, then take out the haunch and hang it out of the sun as long as you can to be sweet, and roast it as you do a haunch of venison; it will eat very fine, especially if the heat will give you leave to keep it long. Take off all the suet before you lay it in the blood, take the other joints and lay them in a large pan, pour over them a quart of red wine and a quart of rape vinegar; lay the fat side of the meat downwards in the pan, (on a hollow tray is best,) and pour the wine and vinegar over it; let it lie twelve hours, then take the neck, breast, and loin out of the pickle; let the shoulder lie a week, if the heat will let you, rub it with bay-salt, saltpetre, and coarse sugar, of each a quarter of an ounce, one handful of common salt, and let it lie a week or ten days: bone the neck, breast, and loin; season them with pepper and salt to your palate, and make a pasty as you do for venison: boil the bones for gravy to fill the pie when it comes out of the oven; and the shoulder boil fresh out of the pickle with a peas-pudding.

And when you cut up the sheep, take the heart, liver,

and lights, boil them a quarter of an hour, then cut them small, and chop them very fine, season them with four large blades of mace, twelve cloves, and a large nutmeg, all beat to powder; chop a pound of suet fine, half a pound of sugar, two pounds of currants clean washed, half a pint of red wine; mix all well together and make a pie; bake it an hour: it is very rich.

## To make Dumplings when you have White Bread

Take the crumb of a two-penny loaf grated fine, as much beef-suet shred as fine as possible, a little salt, half a small nutmeg grated, a large spoonful of sugar, beat two eggs with two spoonfuls of sack; mix all well together, and roll them up as big as a turkey's egg; let the water boil and throw them in: half an hour will boil them. For sauce, melt butter with a little salt, lay the dumplings in a dish, pour the sauce over them, and strew sugar all over the dish.

These are very pretty either at land or sea. You must observe to rub your hands with flour when you make them up.

# IX: Healing Remedies

[I do not pretend to meddle here in the
Physical Way; but a few Directions for the Cook,
or Nurse, I presume, will not be improper, to make
such a Diet, &c, as the Doctor shall order.]

### To make Mutton Broth

Take a pound of loin of mutton, take off the fat, put to it one
quart of water, let it boil and skim it well; then put in a good
piece of upper-crust of bread, and one large blade of mace;
cover it close and let it boil slowly an hour; do not stir it, but
pour the broth clear off; season it with a little salt, and the
mutton will be fit to eat. If you boil turnips, do not boil them
in the broth, but by themselves in another sauce-pan.

### To boil a Scrag of Veal

Set on the scrag in a clean sauce-pan; to each pound of
veal put a quart of water, skim it very clean, then put
in a good piece of upper-crust, a blade of mace to each
pound, and a little parsley tied with a thread; cover it
close; then let it boil very softly two hours, and both
broth and meat will be fit to eat.

### To make Beef-Drink, which is ordered
### for weak People

Take a pound of lean beef, then take off all the fat and
skin, cut it into pieces, put it into a gallon of water with

the under-crust of a penny loaf, and a very little salt; let it boil till it comes to two quarts, then strain it off; and it is a very hearty drink.

## To boil a Chicken

Let your sauce-pan be very clean and nice; when the water boils put in your chicken, which must be very nicely picked and clean, and laid in cold water a quarter of an hour before it is boiled; then take it out of the water boiling, and lay it in a pewter dish; save all the liquor that runs from it in the dish; cut up your chicken all in joints in the dish; then bruise the liver very fine, add a little boiled parsley chopped fine, a very little salt, and a little grated nutmeg; mix it all well together with two spoonfuls of the liquor of the fowl, and pour it into the dish with the rest of the liquor in the dish; if there is not liquor enough, take two or three spoonfuls of the liquor it was boiled in, clap another dish over it; then set it over a chasing-dish of hot coals five or six minutes, and carry it to table hot with the cover on. This is better than butter, and lighter for the stomach, though some choose it only with the liquor, and no parsley nor liver, and that is according to different palates: if it is for a very weak person, take off the skin of the chicken before you set it on the chasing-dish. If you roast it, make nothing but bread-sauce, and that is lighter than any sauce you can make for a weak stomach.

Thus you may dress a rabbit, only bruise but a little piece of the liver.

### To boil a Partridge, or any other Wild Fowl

When your water boils put in your partridge, let it boil ten minutes; then take it up into a pewter plate, and cut it in two, laying the insides next the plate, and have ready some bread-sauce made thus: take the crumb of a halfpenny roll, or thereabouts, and boil it in half a pint of water, with a blade of mace; let it boil two or three minutes, pour away most of the water; then beat it up with a little piece of nice butter, a little salt, and pour it over your partridge; clap a cover over it, then set it over a chasing-dish of coals four or five minutes, and send it away hot, covered close.

Thus you may dress any sort of wild fowl, only boiling it more or less according to the bigness. Ducks, take off the skins before you pour the bread-sauce over them; and if you roast them, lay bread-sauce under them: it is lighter than gravy for weak stomachs.

### To boil a Plaice or Flounder

Let your water boil, throw some salt in; then put in your fish; boil it till you think it is enough, and take it out of the water in a slice to drain; take two spoonfuls of the liquor, with a little salt, a little grated nutmeg; then beat up the yolk of an egg very well with the liquor, and stir in the egg; beat it well together, with a knife carefully slice away all the little bones round the fish, pour the sauce over it; then set it over a chasing-dish of coals for a minute, and send it hot away: or in the room of this sauce, add melted butter in a cup.

## To mince Veal or Chicken for the Sick, or weak People

Mince a chicken, or some veal, very fine, take off the skin; just boil as much water as will moisten it, and no more, with a very little salt, grate a very little nutmeg; then throw a little flour over it, and when the water boils put in the meat; keep shaking it about over the fire a minute; then have ready two or three very thin sippets, toasted nice and brown, laid in the plate, and pour the mince-meat over it.

## To pull a Chicken for the Sick

You must take as much cold chicken as you think proper, take off the skin, and pull the meat into little bits as thick as a quill; then take the bones, boil them with a little salt till they are good, strain it, then take a spoonful of the liquor, a spoonful of milk, a little bit of butter as big as a large nutmeg rolled in flour, a little chopped parsley as much as will lie on a sixpence, and a little salt, if wanted, (this will be enough for half a small chicken,) put all together into the sauce-pan, then keep shaking it till it is thick, and pour it into a hot plate.

## To make White Caudle

You must take two quarts of water, mix in four spoonfuls of oatmeal, a blade or two of mace, a piece of lemon-peel, let it boil, and keep stirring it often: let it boil about a quarter of an hour, and take care it does not boil over; then strain it through a coarse sieve: when you use it, sweeten it to your palate, grate in a little nutmeg, and what wine is proper; and if it is not for a sick person, squeeze in the juice of a lemon.

## To make Water-Gruel

You must take a pint of water and a large spoonful of oatmeal; then stir it together and let it boil up three or four times, stirring it often; do not let it boil over; then strain it through a sieve, salt it to your palate, put in a good piece of fresh butter, brew it with a spoon till the butter is all melted, then it will be fine and smooth, and very good: some love a little pepper in it.

## To boil Sago

Put a large spoonful of sago into three quarters of a pint of water, stir it, and boil it softly till it is as thick as you would have it; then put in wine and sugar, with a little nutmeg to your palate.

## To boil Salop

It is a hard stone ground to powder, and generally sold for one shilling an ounce: take a large tea-spoonful of the powder and put it into a pint of boiling water, keep stirring it till it is like a fine jelly; then put in wine and sugar to your palate, and lemon, if it will agree.

## To make Isinglass Jelly

Take a quart of water, one ounce of isinglass, half an ounce of cloves; boil them to a pint, then strain it upon a pound of loaf-sugar, and when cold sweeten your tea with it; you may make the jelly as above, and leave out the cloves; sweeten to your palate, and add a little wine.

### To make the Pectoral Drink

Take a gallon of water and half a pound of pearl-barley, boil it with a quarter of a pound of figs split, a pennyworth of liquorice sliced to pieces, a quarter of a pound of raisins of the sun stoned; boil all together till half is wasted, then strain it off. This is ordered in the measles, and several other disorders, for a drink.

### To make Buttered Water, or what the Germans call Egg-Soup, who are very fond of it for Supper

Take a pint of water, beat up the yolk of an egg with the water, put in a piece of butter as big as a small walnut, two or three knobs of sugar, and keep stirring it all the time it is on the fire; when it begins to boil, bruise it between the sauce-pan and a mug till it is smooth and has a great froth; then it is fit to drink. This is ordered in a cold, or where eggs will agree with the stomach.

### To make Seed-Water

Take a spoonful of coriander-seed, half a spoonful of caraway-seed, bruised and boiled in a pint of water; then strain it, and bruise it with the yolk of an egg: mix it with sack and double-refined sugar, according to your palate.

### To make Bread-Soup for the Sick

Take a quart of water, set it on the fire in a clean saucepan, and as much dry crust of bread cut to pieces as the top of a penny loaf (the drier the better) a bit of butter as big as a walnut; let it boil, then beat it with a spoon, and keep boiling it till the bread and water is well mixed; then season it with a very little salt, and it is a pretty thing for a weak stomach.

## To make artificial Asses Milk

Take two ounces of pearl-barley, two large spoonfuls of hartshorn shavings, one ounce of eringo-root, one ounce of China-root, one ounce of preserved ginger, eighteen snails bruised with the shells, to be boiled in three quarts of water till it comes to three pints, then boil a pint of new milk, mix it with the rest, and put in two ounces of balsam of Tolu. Take half a pint in the morning, and half a pint at night.

## To make Barley-Water

Put a quarter of a pound of pearl-barley into two quarts of water, let it boil, skim it very clean, boil half away, and strain it off; sweeten to your palate, but not too sweet, and put in two spoonfuls of white wine; drink it luke-warm.

## To make Sage-Tea

Take a little sage, a little baum, put it into a pan, slice a lemon, peel and all, a few knobs of sugar, one glass of white wine, pour on these two or three quarts of boiling water, cover it, and drink when thirsty; when you think it strong enough of the herbs, take them out, otherwise it will make it bitter.

### To make it for a Child
A little sage, baum, rue, mint, and penny-royal, pour boiling water on, and sweeten to your palate.

### Liquor for a Child that has the Thrush
Take half a pint of spring-water, a knob of double-refined sugar, a very little bit of alum, beat it well together with the yolk of an egg, then beat it in a large spoonful of the juice of sage; tie a rag to the end of a stick, dip it in this liquor, and often clean the mouth. Give the child over night one drop of laudanum, and the next day proper physic, washing the mouth often with the liquor.

### To boil Comfrey-Roots
Take a pound of comfrey-roots, scrape them clean, cut them into little pieces, and put them into three pints of water, let them boil till there is about a pint, then strain it, and when it is cold put it into a sauce-pan; if there is any settling at the bottom, throw it away; mix it with sugar to your palate, add half a pint of mountain wine and the juice of a lemon, let it boil, then pour it into a clean earthen pot, and set it by for use. Some boil it with milk, and it is very good where it will agree, and is reckoned a very great strengthener.

### To make the Knuckle Broth
Take twelve shank-ends of a leg of mutton, break them well and soak them in cold spring-water for an hour, then take a small brush and scour them clean with warm water and salt, then put them into two quarts of spring-water and let them simmer till reduced to one quart;

when they have been on one hour, put in one ounce of hartshorn-shavings and the bottom of a halfpenny-roll; be careful to take the scum off as it rises; when done, strain it off, and if any fat remains, take it off with a knife when cold; drink a quarter of a pint warm when you go to bed, and one hour before you rise: it is a certain restorative at the beginning of a decline, or when any weakness is the complaint.

*N. B.* If it is made right, it is the colour of calf's foot jelly, and is strong enough to bear a spoon upright. [From the College of Physicians, London.]

## A Medicine for a Disorder in the Bowels

Take an ounce of beef-suet, half a pint of milk, and half a pint of water, mix together with a table-spoonful of wheat-flour, put it over the fire ten minutes, and keep it stirring all the time; and take a coffee-cupful two or three times a-day.

## A certain Cure for the Bite of a Mad Dog

Let the patient be blooded at the arm nine or ten ounces. Take of the herb called in Latin *lichen cinereus terrestris*, in English, ash-coloured ground liverwort, cleaned, dried, and powdered, half an ounce. Of black pepper, powdered, two drachms. Mix these well together, and divide the powder into four doses, one of which must be taken every morning fasting, for four mornings successively, in half a pint of cow's milk warm. After these four doses are taken, the patient must go into the cold bath, or a cold spring or river every morning salting for a month. He must be dipped all over, but not to stay in (with his head above water) longer than half a minute, if the water be very cold. After this he must go in three times a week for a fortnight longer.

N. B. – The lichen is a very common herb, and grows generally in sandy and barren soils all over England. The right time to gather it is in the months of October and November. [*D. Mead.*]

### Another Cure for the Bite of a Mad Dog

For the bite of a mad dog, for either man or beast, take six ounces of rue clean picked and bruised, four ounces of garlic peeled and bruised, four ounces of Venice treacle, and four ounces of filed pewter, or scraped tin. Boil these in two quarts of the best ale, in a pan covered close, over a gentle fire, for the space of an hour; then strain the ingredients from the liquor. Give eight or nine spoonfuls of it warm to a man, or a woman, three mornings fasting. Eight or nine spoonfuls is sufficient for the strongest; a lesser quantity to those younger, or of a weaker constitution, as you may judge of their strength. Ten or twelve spoonfuls for a horse or a bullock; three, four, or five to a sheep, hog, or dog. This must be given within nine days after the bite: it seldom fails in man or beast. If you bind some of the ingredients on the wound, it will be so much the better.

### Receipt against the Plague

Take of rue, sage, mint, rosemary, wormwood, and lavender, a handful of each; infuse them together in a gallon of white wine vinegar, put the whole into a stone pot, closely covered up, upon warm wood-ashes for four days, after which draw off (or strain through fine flannel) the liquid, and put it into bottles well corked; and into every quart bottle put a quarter of an ounce of camphor: with this preparation wash your mouth, and rub your loins and your temples every day; snuff a little up your nostrils when you go into the air, and carry about you a bit of spunge dipped in the same, in order to smell to upon all occasions, especially when you are near any place or person that is infected. They write, that four malefactors, (who had robbed the infected houses, and murdered the people during the course of the plague,) owned, when they came to the gallows, that they had preserved themselves from the contagion by using the above medicine only: and that they went the whole time from house to house without any fear of the distemper.

### For a Consumption; an approved Receipt, by a Lady at Paddington

Take the yolk of a new laid egg, beat it up well with three large spoonfuls of rose water; mix it well in half a pint of new milk from the cow, sweeten it well with sirup de capillaire, and grate some nutmeg in it. Drink it every morning fasting for a month, and resrain from spirituous liquors of any kind.

### To stop a violent Purging, or the Flux

Take a third part of a gill of the very best double distilled anise-seeds; grate a third part of a large nutmeg into it. To be taken the same quantity an hour after breakfast, one hour after dinner, and, if occasion, an hour before going to bed.

## For Obstructions in Females

Succotorine aloes, one ounce; cardamum-feed, a quarter of an ounce; snake root, a quarter of an ounce; gum-myrrh, a quarter of an ounce; saffron, a quarter of an ounce; cochineal, two scruples; zedoary, two scruples; rhubarb, two scruples: let these drugs be well beaten in a mortar, and put them into a large bottle; add thereto a pint and a half of mountain wine; place it near the fire for the space of three days and nights, shaking it often. Let the patient take a small tea-cup-full twice a week in the morning, an hour before rising.

## For a Hoarseness

Two ounces of pennyroyal-water, the yolk of a new laid egg beaten, thirty drops of cochineal, twenty drops of oil of anise-feed, mixed well and sweetened with white sugar candy. A large spoonful to be taken night and morning.

## Lozenges for the Heart-burn

Take one pound of chalk, beat it to a powder in a mortar, with one pound and a half of white loaf-sugar, and one ounce of bole-ammoniac; mix them well together, and put in something to moisten them, to make it of a proper consistency or paste; make them into small lozenges, and let them lie in a band-box on the top of an oven a week or more to dry, shaking the box sometimes.

## Lozenges for a Cold

Take two pounds of common white loaf-sugar, beat it well in a mortar, dissolve six ounces of Spanish liquorice in a little warm water; one ounce of gum-arabic dissolved likewise; add thereto a little oil of anise-seed; mix them well to a proper consistency, and cut them into small lozenges; let them lie in a band box on the top of an oven a considerable time to dry, shaking the box sometimes.

## The genuine Receipt to make
## Turlington's Balsam

Balsam of Peru, one ounce; best storax, two ounces; benjamin, impregnated with sweet almonds, three ounces; aloes Succotorine, myrrh elect, purest frankincense, roots of angelica, flowers of St. John's wort, of each of these half an ounce; beat the drugs well in a mortar, and put them into a large glass bottle; add thereto a pint, or rather more, of the best spirits of wine, and let the bottle stand by the kitchen fire, or in the chimney-corner, two days and two nights; then decant it off in small bottles for use, and let them be well corked and sealed.

N. B. The same quantity of spirits of wine poured on the ingredients, letting them stand by the fire, or in some warm place for the space of six days and nights, will serve for common use; pour off the same in small bottles, and let them be well corked and sealed.

# X: Soaps and Scents

### To make Red, Light, or Purple Wash-Balls

Get some white soap, beat it in a mortar; then put it into a pan, and cover it down close; let the same be put into a copper, so that the water does not come to the top of the pan; then cover your copper as close as you can, to stop the steam; make the water boil some time; take the pan out, and beat it well with a wooden stirrer till it is all melted with the heat of the water; then pour it out into drops, and cut them into square pieces as small as a walnut; let it lie three days on an oven in a band-box; afterwards put them into a pan, and damp them with rose-water, mash it well with your hands, and mould them according to your fancy, viz. squeeze them as hard and as close as you possibly can; make them very round, and put them into a band-box or a sieve two or three days; then scrape them a little with a wash-ball scraper (which are made for that purpose), and let them lie eight or nine days; afterwards scrape them very smooth and to your mind.

N. B. If you would have them red, when you first mash them, put in a little vermilion; if light, some hair-powder; and if purple, some rose-pink.

### White Almond Wash Balls

Take some white soap and slice it thin, put it into a band-box on the top of an oven to dry, three weeks or more;

when it is dry, beat it in a mortar till it is a powder; to every four ounces of soap add one ounce of hair-powder, half an ounce of white-lead; put them into a pan, and damp them with rose-water to make it of a proper consistency; make them into balls as hard and close as possible, scrape them with a ball-scraper, and use the same process as before-mentioned, letting them lie three weeks in a sieve to dry; then finish them with a ball-scraper to your mind.

### Windsor Soap – Two shillings per Pound

Get some of the whitest soap, shave it into thin slices; melt it in a stew-pan over a slow fire, and scent it very strong with oil of carraways; pour it into a drawer made for that purpose; let it stand three days or more, and cut it into square pieces to your fancy.

### To make Lip Salve

Take half a pound of hog's lard, put it into a pan, with one ounce and a half of virgin-wax; let it stand on a slow fire till it is melted; then take a small tin-pot, and fill it with water, and put therein some alkanet-root; let it boil till it is of a fine red colour; then strain some of it, and mix it with the ingredients according to your fancy, and scent it with essence of lemon; pour it into small boxes, and smooth the top with your finger.

N. B. – You may pour a little out first, to see if it is of a proper colour to your fancy.

### French Rouge – Five Shillings per Pot

Take some carmine, and mix it with hair-powder to make it as pale as you please, according to your fancy.

## Opiate for the Teeth – Two Shillings and Sixpence per Pot

Take one pound of honey, let it be very well boiled and skimmed, a quarter of a pound of bole-ammoniac, one ounce of dragon's-blood, one ounce of oil of sweet almonds, half an ounce of oil of cloves, eight drops of essence of bergamot, one gill of honey-water; mix all well together, and pour it into pots for use.

## Delescot's Opiate

Half an ounce of bole-ammoniac, one ounce of powder of myrrh, one ounce of dragon's-blood, half an ounce of orrice-root, half an ounce of roch-alum, half an ounce of ground ginger, two ounces of honey; mix all well together, and put it in pots for use.

## Tooth-Powder – One Shilling per Bottle

Burn some roch-alum, and beat it in a mortar, sift it fine; then take some rose-pink, and mix them well together to make it of a pale red colour; add thereto a little powder of myrrh, and put it into bottles for use.

## To make Shaving-Oil – One Shilling per Bottle

Dissolve a quantity of oil-soap, cut it into thin slices, in spirits of wine; let it stand a week, then put in as much soft-soap till the liquor becomes of a clammy substance: scent as you please, and bottle it for use.

## To make Shaving-Powder

Take some white-soap, and shave it in very thin slices; let it be well dried on the top of an oven in a band box;

beat it in a mortar till it is very fine, sift it through a fine sieve, and scent it as you please.

## Soap to fill Shaving-Boxes

Take some of the whitest soap, beat it in a mortar, and scent it with oil of carraways, make it flat; then chop in some vermilion, or powder blue, to marble it, with a very thin knife dipt in the same; double it up, and squeeze it hard into the boxes; then scrape it smooth with a knife.

## Wash for the Face

Take one quart of milk, a quarter of a pound of salt-petre beaten to a powder; put in two pennyworth of oil of anise-seed, one pennyworth of oil of cloves, about four thimbles full of the best white wine vinegar; put it into a bottle, and let it stand in sand half-way up, in the sun, or in some warm place for a fortnight without the cork; afterwards cork and seal it up.

## How to make Almond Milk
## for a Wash

Take five ounces of bitter almonds, blanch them and beat them in a marble mortar very fine; you may put in a spoonful of sack when you beat them; then take the whites of three new-laid eggs, three pints of spring-water, and one pint of sack. Mix them all very well together; then strain it through a fine cloth, and put it into a bottle, and keep it for use. You may put in lemon, or powder of pearl, when you make use of it.

## An approved Method practised by Mrs. Dukely, the Queen's Tire-Woman, to preserve Hair, and make it grow thick

Take one quart of white wine, put in one handful of rosemary flowers, half a pound of honey, distil them together; then add a quarter of a pint of oil of sweet almonds, shake it very well together, put a little of it into a cup, warm it blood-warm, rub it well on your head, and comb it dry.

## A Stick to take Hair out

Take two ounces and a half of rosin, and one ounce of bees-wax; melt them together, and make them into sticks for use.

## Liquid for the Hair. – Two Shillings a Quarter of a Pint

To three quarts of sweet-oil, put a quarter of a pound of alkanet-root, cut in small pieces; let it be boiled some time over a steam; add thereto three ounces of oil of jessamine, and one ounce of oil of lavender; strain it through a coarse cloth, but do not squeeze it.

## Sweet-scented Bags to lay with Linen – At one Shilling and Sixpence, Two Shillings and Sixpence, &c. &c. &c. each Bag

Eight ounces of coriander-seeds, eight ounces of sweet orrice root, eight ounces of damask-rose leaves, eight ounces of calamus-aromaticus, one ounce of mace, one ounce of cinnamon, half an ounce of cloves, four drachms of musk powder, two drachms of white loaf-sugar, three ounces of lavender-flowers, and some Roduam wood, beat them well together, and sew them up in small silk bags.

## Orange-Butter
Melt a small quantity of spermaceti in sweet-oil, and put in a little fine Dutch pink to colour it; then add a little oil of orange to scent it; and lastly, while it is very hot, put in some spirits of wine to curdle it.

## Marechalle Powder, Sixteen Shillings per Pound
One ounce of cloves, one ounce of mace, one ounce of cinnamon, beat them very well to a fine powder, add to them four pounds of hair-powder, and half a pound of Spanish burnt amber beaten very fine, a quarter of an ounce of oil of lavender, half an ounce of oil of thyme, a quarter of an ounce of essence of amber, five drops of oil of laurel, a quarter of an ounce of oil of sassafras; mix them all well together.

## Virgin's Milk – Two Shillings per Bottle
Put one ounce of tincture of benjamin into a pint of cold water: mix it well, and let it stand one day; then run it through a flannel-bag with some tow in it; put it in bottles for use.

## Honey-Water – One Shilling per Bottle
One quart of rectified spirits of wine, two drachms of tincture of ambergrease, two drachms of tincture of musk, half a pint of water; filter it according to your fancy, and put it into small bottles.

## Milk Flude Water

One quart of spirits of wine, half an ounce of oil of cloves, one drachm of essence of lemons, fifteen drops of oil of Rhodium, a little cochineal in powder, to colour it of a fine pink; let it stand one day, then filter it, but with no water.

## Miss in her Teens

One quart of spirits of wine; essence of bergamot, one ounce; oil of Rhodium, two drachms; tincture of musk, half a drachm, and half a pint of water; mix them well together, and put them into bottles for use.

## Lady Lilley's Ball

Take twelve ounces of oil-soap shaved very fine, spermaceti three ounces, melt them together; two ounces of bizmuth dissolved in rose-water for the space of three hours, one ounce of oil of thyme, one ounce of the oil of carraways, one ounce of essence of lemons; mix all well together.

## Nun's Cream

One ounce of pearl-powder, twenty drops of oil of Rhodium, and two ounces of fine pomatum; mix all well together.

## Cold Cream

Take one pint of trotter-oil, a quarter of a pound of hog's-lard, one ounce of spermaceti, a bit of virgin-wax; warm them together with a little rose-water, and beat it up with a whisk.

## The Ambrosia Nosegay

Take one pint of spirits of wine, one drachm of oil of cloves, one ounce of oil of nutmegs; mix them, and filter it as you please.

## Eau de Bouquet

Take one quart of spirits of wine, half an ounce of musk, two drachms of tincture of saffron, mix them well together, and let them stand one day; then filter it with any water.

## Eau de Luce

Two ounces of the best rectified spirits of wine, one drachm of oil of amber, two drachms of salt of tartar, prepared powder of amber two drachms, twenty drops of oil of nutmegs; put them all into a bottle, and shake it well; let it stand five hours, then filter it, and always keep it by you, and when you would make *eau de luce*, put it into the strongest spirits of sal-ammoniac.

## Hard Pomatum

Take three pounds of mutton-suet, boil and skim it well till it is quite clear, pour it off from the dross which remains at the bottom; then add thereto eight ounces of virgin-wax, melt them together, and scent it with essence of lemon; make it into rolls according to fancy.

## To make Sirop de Capillarie

Put seven pounds of common lump-sugar into a pan, and thereto add seven pints of water; boil it well, and keep skimming it; then take the white of an egg, put it in some water, and beat it up well with a whisk: take the froth off and scatter it therein, and keep it skimming until it is quite clear; then add thereto half a pint of orange-flower-water; mix it well together, let it stand till cold, and put it into a stone bottle, or in bottles for use, let them be quite clean and dry before it is put into them, otherwise it will make it mothery and spoil it.

*N. B.* – If you chuse to have it of a high colour, burn a little sugar in a pan, of a brown colour; afterwards put a little capillaire thereto, stir it about with a wooden spoon, and mix it well with the capillaire according to your fancy.

### To make Dragon-Roots

Take some mallow-roots, skin them, and pick one end with a pin or needle till you have made it like a brush; then take some powder of brasil, and some cochineal, boil them together, and put in the roots till you think they are thoroughly dyed; then take them out, and lay them by the fire to dry.

# XI: Housekeeping

### How to keep clear from Bugs

First take out of your room all silver and gold lace, then set the chairs about the room, shut up your windows and doors, sack a blanket over each window, and before the chimney, and over the doors of the room, set open all closets and cupboard doors, all your drawers and boxes, hang the rest of your bedding on the chair-backs, lay the feather-bed on a table, then set a large broad earthen pan in the middle of the room, and in that set a chasing dish that stands on feet, full of charcoal well lighted; if your room is very bad, a pound of rolled brimstone; if only a few, half a pound; lay it on the charcoal, and get out of the room as quick as possibly you can, or it will take away your breath: shut your door close, with the blanket over it, and be sure to set it so as nothing can catch fire: if you have any India pepper, throw it in with the brimstone. You must take great care to have the door open whilst you lay in the brimstone, that you may get out as soon as possible. Do not open the door under six hours, and then you must be very careful how you go in to open the windows: then brush and sweep your room very clean; wash it well with boiling lee, or boiling water with a little unslacked lime in it; get a pint of spirits of wine, a pint of spirits of turpentine, and an ounce of camphire, shake all well together, and with a bunch of feathers wash your bedstead very well, and sprinkle the rest over the feather-bed and about the room.

If you find great swarms about the room, and some not dead, do this over again, and you will be quite clear. Every spring and fall wash your bedstead with half a pint, and you will never have a bug; but if you find any come in with new goods or boxes, &c. only wash your bedstead, and sprinkle all over your bedding and bed, and you will be clear; but be sure to do it as soon as you find one. If your room is very bad, it will be well to paint the room after the brimstone is burnt in it.

This never fails, if rightly done.

### An effectual Way to clear your Bedstead of Bugs

Take quicksilver and mix it well in a mortar with the white of an egg till the quicksilver is all well mixed, and there are no bubbles; then beat up some white of an egg very fine, and mix with the quicksilver till it is like a fine ointment, then with a feather anoint the bedstead all over in every creek and corner, and about the lacing and binding, where you think there is any. Do this two or three times: it is a certain cure, and will not spoil any thing.

### Directions *to the* Housemaid

Always when you sweep a room, throw a little wet sand all over it, and that will gather up all the flew and dust, prevent it from rising, clean the boards, and save the bedding, pictures, and all other furniture from dust or dirt.

## How to make Yellow Varnish

Take a quart of spirit of wine, and put to it eight ounces of sandarach, shake it half an hour; next day it will be fit for use, but strain it first: take lamp-black, and put in your varnish about the thickness of a pancake; mix it well, but stir it not too salt; then do it eight times over, and let it stand still the next day; then take some burnt ivory, and oil of turpentine as fine as butter; then mix it with some of your varnish, till you have varnished it fit for polishing; then polish it with tripoly in fine flour; then lay it on the wood smooth, with one of the brushes, then let it dry, and do it so eight times at the least; when it is very dry, lay on your varnish that is mixed, and when it is dry, polish it with a wet cloth dipped in tripoly, and rub it as hard as you would do platters.

## How to make a pretty Varnish to colour little Baskets, Bowls, or any Board where nothing hot is set on

Take either red, black, or white wax, which colour you want to make; to every two ounces of sealing-wax one ounce of spirit of wine, pound the wax fine, then sift it through a fine lawn sieve till you have made it extremely fine; put it into a large phial with the spirits of wine, shake it, let it stand within the air of the fire forty-eight hours, shaking it often; then with a little brush rub your baskets all over with it; let it dry, and do it over a second time, and it makes them look very pretty.

## How to clean Gold and Silver Lace

Take alabaster finely beaten and searced, and put it into an earthen pipkin, and set it upon a chasing-dish of coals, and let it boil for some time, stirring it often with a stick first; when it begins to boil, it will be very heavy; when it is enough, you will find it in the stirring very light; then take it off the fire, lay your lace upon a piece of flannel, and strew your powder upon it; knock it well in with a hard cloth brush; when you think it is enough, brush the powder out with a clean brush.

### To clean White Sattins, Flowered Silks with Gold and Silver in them

Take stale bread crumbled very fine, mixed with powder-blue, rub it very well over the silk or sattin; then shake it well, and with clean soft cloths dust it well: if any gold or silver flowers, afterwards take a piece of crimson in grain velvet, and rub the flowers with it.

### To keep Arms, Iron, or Steel, from rusting

Take the filings of lead, or dust of lead, finely beaten in an iron mortar, putting to it oil of spike, which will make the iron smell well; and if you oil your arms, or any thing that is made of iron or steel, you may keep them in moist airs from rusting.

### To take Iron-molds out of Linen

Take sorrel, bruise it well in a mortar, squeeze it through a cloth, bottle it, and keep it for use: take a little of the above juice, in a silver or tin sauce-pan, boil it over a lamp; as it boils dip in the iron-mold, do not rub it, but only squeeze it; as soon as the iron-mold is out, throw it into cold water.

## To take Iron-molds out of Linen, and Grease
## out of Woollen or Silk – One Shilling a Bottle

Take four ounces of spirits of turpentine, and one ounce of essence of lemon; mix them well together, and put it into bottles for use.

## To prevent the Insection among
## Horned Cattle

Make an issue in the dewlap, put in a peg of black hellebore, and rub all the vents both behind and before with tar.

GREATFOOD

## A TASTE OF THE SUN

*Elizabeth David*

LEGENDARY COOK AND WRITER Elizabeth David
changed the way Britain ate, introducing a postwar nation
to the sun-drenched delights of the Mediterranean, and
bringing new flavours and aromas such as garlic,
wine and olive oil into its kitchens.

This mouthwatering selection of her writings and
recipes embraces the richness of French and Italian cuisine,
from earthy cassoulets to the simplest spaghetti, as well as
evoking the smell of buttered toast, the colours of foreign
markets and the pleasures of picnics. Rich with anecdote,
David's writing is defined by a passion for good, authentic,
well-balanced food that still inspires chefs today.

*'Above all, Elizabeth David's books
make you want to cook'*
TERENCE CONRAN